CHRISTIAN
Tears of Pakistan

FALSELY ACCUSED
Under Blasphemy Law 295-BC

AMEER

CHRISTIAN

Tears of Pakistan
FALSELY ACCUSED
Under Blasphemy Law 295-BC

Copyright © 2020 Ameer

All rights reserved. This book is protected under the copyright laws of the United States of America. This book may not be copied or reprinted for commercial gain or profit. The use of short quotations or occasional page copying for personal or group study is permitted and encouraged. Permission will be granted on request.

This book is a compilation of news stories and articles of incidents that have taken place in Pakistan from the time of the installation of the blasphemy law, 295-BC. Most of the pages in this book are taken from different online sources. The sources are given credit where possible, but many of the credits are missing due to the loss of data. I want to thank all of the resourceful websites and media for making this book possible. (The true identity of the author is being withheld for his protection.)

Paperback: ISBN: 978-1-943523-75-7

LAURUS BOOKS
A DIVISION OF THE LAURUS COMPANY, INC.
www.TheLaurusCompany.com

This book may be purchased in paperback from TheLaurusCompany.com, Amazon, and other retailers around the world. May also be available in formats for electronic readers from their respective stores.

Pastor Ameer is an amazing man of God. I am very impressed with his pure faith and courage, which makes him bold enough to overcome any persecution in the name of Jesus Christ. I am certain we will see the rapid expansion of his ministry in the near future because of his outstanding God-given intelligence and wisdom with a genuinely humble heart. I pray his book may be read throughout the world, and his love of Pakistani Christians may bring forth abundant fruits.

 —**Young Kim, M.D.**
 Orthopaedic Surgeon, Korea

Christians living in the West cannot begin to imagine what life is like for Christians in the Islamic nation of Pakistan, where Christians make up just 1.5 percent of the population and, as Dr. Ameer explains, on a regular basis, they endure incidents "of social discrimination, land theft, sexual harassment, church attacks, hate mongering, and discrimination in educational institutions." Christians can be beaten by mobs or put to death by the government for allegedly insulting Islam. They are deprived of good jobs, pushed into the slums, into demeaning lifelong work with little hope for their children. Young women can be kidnapped, forcibly converted to Islam, and then married off to older men. This is normal life for our brothers and sisters there, and I am thankful to Dr. Ameer for taking the time to share this story with the outside world. But there is light in the midst of the darkness, and this book will not only burden you. It will help you stand with your spiritual family in Pakistan, where the name of Jesus will one day be greatly exalted.

 —**Dr. Michael L. Brown**, President
 FIRE School of Ministry
 Host, *Line of Fire* radio broadcast

I am thrilled to recommend this book. It is a great help to understand the history and issues of the church and Christians in Pakistan. We are blessed to now have such a comprehensive understanding of the mindset of believers and Christian workers there. It should be spread to everyone who is working or considering working in the Middle East as well as the country of Pakistan.

 —**Eddie Wilson**
 Founder and President
 Christian Media International

I first met Ameer at a prayer conference in Atlanta, Georgia. He was one of the speakers, and as he spoke about Pakistan and the persecution Christians face, I was moved by his commitment to Christ and his love for his nation. Since that time, I've had Ameer stay in my home and preach in my church, and the same humble, sincere, and committed follower of Christ that I saw in him as a speaker is exactly what I saw in his life in our time of personal fellowship. You will be blessed by his book and challenged to a deeper commitment to following Jesus, regardless of the cost.

>—**Jonathan Morgan**, Senior Pastor
>Cornerstone Church International, Inc.
>Raleigh, NC

Reading this incredibly compelling work of Pastor Ameer, my heart has been so stirred to pray for Christ's people, my brothers and sisters in Pakistan. We are charged to rejoice with those who rejoice and weep with those who weep. Christian Tears Of Pakistan *will compel Christians to go beyond weeping with the horribly persecuted church there, but to rise up in strong intercession, that their faith will not fail in this hour of intense trial! WE MUST wage war with the god of this world who is still effectively blinding and poisoning these unbelieving minds with demonic hatred toward those who actually love them! May their suffering be rewarded with a mighty outpouring of salvations in the Muslim world, for whom Jesus bled and died! This is a must-read for every disciple of Jesus Christ!*

>—**Tom Anglin**, Senior Pastor
>The Bridge Church of WNC
>Spruce Pine, NC

I first met Ameer five years ago. He has a very interesting background. I know he is a godly man. God is using him greatly in Pakistan for a mission, and I have no doubt. This book is not for the Pakistani Christians. They have tears because they love Jesus, and this book challenges us to love Jesus as Pakistani Christians do. This touched my heart when I asked the question of myself from time to time, what have I done for Jesus. This book will challenge everybody who will read it. Their condition is worse than ours, but they don't complain. They do what they can do their best. I want to congratulate brothers and sister who live in Pakistan. I strongly want him to translate this book into

Korean. When we meet Jesus, they will have endorsement from Jesus, and God will love to see them. Lastly, I want to congratulate Pastor Ameer. Please read this book. This book will help you, and every Korean should read this book.

> —**Dr. John C. Kim,** Senior Pastor
> Charlotte Bethel Korean Church
> Charlotte, NC, USA

I trust this book will be a blessing to all those who love the church.

For we preach not ourselves, but Christ Jesus the Lord; and ourselves your servants for Jesus' sake. For God, who commanded the light to shine out of darkness, hath shined in our hearts, to give the light of the knowledge of the glory of God in the face of Jesus Christ. But we have this treasure in earthen vessels, that the excellency of the power may be of God, and not of us.
2 Corinthians 4:5-7.

> —**John Fullerton MacArthur, Jr.**
> Pastor/author/internationally
> syndicated Christian teaching
> radio program "Grace to You."
> Pastor-teacher Grace Community Church
> Sun Valley, CA

Our ministry, Vision International University, has had the privilege of translating materials and planting Bible colleges in Pakistan since the 1990s. Without a doubt, God is moving in that great nation, in spite of the true hardships and persecution experienced by our brothers and sisters there. Most Western Christians are unaware of the suffering of our family in Pakistan, and I am glad to see a book written by a Pakistani pastor who can share with clarity what is actually happening in this part of the world. Reading it will doubtless touch, or hopefully break, your heart and move the reader to prayer and action for the church in Pakistan.

> —**Stan E. DeKoven, Ph.D.,** President
> Vision International University

I know thy works, and tribulation, and poverty, (but thou art rich) and I know the blasphemy of them which say they are Jews, and are not, but are the synagogue of Satan.

Fear none of those things which thou shalt suffer: behold, the devil shall cast some of you into prison, that ye may be tried; and ye shall have tribulation ten days: be thou faithful unto death, and I will give thee a crown of life.

He that hath an ear, let him hear what the Spirit saith unto the churches; He that overcometh shall not be hurt of the second death.

Revelation 2:9-11 KJV

TABLE OF CONTENTS

Introduction 9

Part 1: The Persecution of Christians 17

Part 2: Introduction to Pakistan from
        Christian Point of View 53

Part 3: Blasphemy Law and its Effects on
        Pakistani Christians 61

Part 4: International Humanitarian Organizations
        Working in Pakistan 97

Part 5: Worship in the Valley of the
        Shadow of Death 104

Conclusion 117

Final Words 125

Bibliography 127

CHRISTIAN TEARS OF PAKISTAN
Under Blasphemy Law 295-BC

INTRODUCTION

I was born in a Christian family. I am fourth generation Christian. My great grandparents accepted Jesus Christ through the Presbyterian American missionaries. They were formerly idol worshipers. They were the lowest caste Hindus (untouchable people) whom missionaries approached to share the gospel. As far as I know, they used to eat dead animals as well, but American missionaries brought them to Jesus Christ.

I was saved on August 31, 1999. On that day, I accepted Jesus Christ as my Lord and Savior and decided to give my life to Him for His work. In the four generations of my Christian family, I was the first person to become a pastor. I am delighted by the fact that the Lord chose me to serve Him. In my family, nobody studied, even until high school. But it was God's plan for me, and He prepared me for His work. I have been in ministry since 2001. God has been very faithful to me through this entire journey. Even though it has been extremely difficult, I felt His presence with me. In the past, even though I faced severe persecution and mob justice in my area for two months, I was able to maintain my faith toward God through His power.

Every morning in Public School I had to recite a Muslim prayer in assembly. I remember when I was a small child, and even when I grew up as a young man, my father and grandfather were poor farmers. They were used to work for Chaudhry, or head of village who owned agricultural land. My father and grandfather had their own glasses or bowls for drinking water and buttermilk (Lassi). They were treated as untouchables and were not allowed to touch the water jug and glasses of the Muslim owner. I always saw him giving them bread (Roti) not in a plate but in their hands, and they never sat near the main eating bowl. They had to sit at a distance. I also ate bread and drank water or buttermilk and yogurt shakes (lassi) like that. This severe kind of discrimination against Christians I have seen in Pakistan. Maybe this kind of hatred is not as much in big cities now, but in remote villages, it is still going on.

Being a Christian is not an easy task in Pakistan, and it is more so for the leaders and pastors. When some minor mistakes are done by the Christians toward the Muslim brothers, it becomes very hard for all Christian communities due to their attitudes toward us. For example, whole Christian communities suffered when a Christian boy was accused of burning Quran in 2011. He was charged with committing blasphemy under Law 295-BC. I have experienced the risky day-to-day life and faced the aggressive and charged mobs who stone and burn churches and houses and kill Christians.

As a Pakistani, I love my country. Pakistan is a great country, but it is neither easy nor safe to live there when you are a Christian. In Pakistan, Christians face new challenges every day. There is rejection, hatred, and discrimination toward Christians, who are considered second- or third-class citizens. Even a lowest grade Muslim is more powerful in Pakistan than any Christian, as we are always living under a threat hoping that nobody accuses us of blasphemy falsely. A sense of insecurity and uncertainty is always chasing us.

As a Christian, I do not feel safe because it is very easy to target us due to hatred toward Jesus Christ and His followers. Even if I do no wrong toward the people and the society due to my faith, it can spring a personal hatred, and they can charge me under the blasphemy law. The brutal fact is that even though there will be no proof that I committed the blasphemy, there will be many people who will be ready to witness against me falsely.

Just one announcement from an Imam in a mosque's loudspeaker will provoke a whole community, and an aggressive mob will come out to kill and burn Christians and set up a court or do justice on the road. I always feel, *Am I an alien in my own country*? I am not safe in Pakistan, as Muslims claim that Pakistan is for Muslims and was made for that purpose. The fate of Christians in Pakistan is to live under a constant threat of persecutions that sometimes can lead to death. Ironically, the world also treats us in a similar fashion, thinking that if we are from Pakistan, we are also terrorists.

In a way, we Pakistani Christians have no place on this planet. Pakistanis think that America and the West are Christian, so whenever something happens against Islam in America or the West, Christians have to pay the price in Pakistan. Pakistanis consider that Christians who live in Pakistan are also responsible because America and the West are Christians. Even though Pakistani Christians love Pakistan more than anyone else and have never been involved in any anti-Pakistani activity, they always become the target of many.

Burning Christian houses, persecution, and killing have become a constant threat for Christians in Pakistan. This is the reason many Christians have fled from Pakistan and are trying to seek asylum through UNHCR, the UN refugee agency in Sri Lanka, Malaysia, Thailand, but their life is miserable there because they are waiting for their application to be processed. Videos can be seen on YouTube and news can be read about asylum seekers' lives and how these refugees are having to live there. We pray for the peace and protection of Pakistan and the Christians who live there. Long live Pakistan.

Everyday Question

There is a very common question that has been asked of me, and I think it is asked of the majority of Pakistani Christians wherever they work in Pakistan, especially women who work in houses and men who work in factories with Muslim friends. When Muslims see or spend some time with a Christian, they ask him or her, "You are very good man (or woman); why do you not become Muslim or accept Islam? You will go to heaven." They think all people who are not Muslims are KAFIR (Non Believer).

I once went to the court, not for any crime but just to accompanied a friend. I met a Muslim friend there. He was a good person, and he was an employee in court. We talked about my life, and then he told me, "You are an educated man. I want to invite you (Daawat) to Islam. Christianity is an old religion. Bible has been changed, and Christianity is no more relevant." My answer to that Muslim friend was, "Old is Gold." I respect you, but I thank God that I am Christian. I always tell people I respect Muslims and Muslim friends, but if you talk about my faith, then I am follower of Jesus. Respecting does not mean I must follow your faith. I have unshaken faith in Jesus that He is my "Lord and Savior" and the Son of God who became man so that the sons of man can be sons of God.

There are more interesting stories. When I visited the USA the first time, I met a Pakistani Muslim in Miami, Florida. He was very kind to me. We were so glad to meet each other. After some time, he gave me an invitation to become Muslim and study the Quran,. I told him, "I am a Christian, and I respect you and your faith. However, I believe, and it is historical fact, that we Christians have made this world a beautiful place. This is the reason you are here in America, a country that has Christian roots. I cannot see any better religion than Christianity. This is what I feel and believe as a Christian. I am not against any religion, but this is my belief. You should study Christianity."

In every corner of Pakistan, a person like me who is a pastor is motivated every day, and sometimes forced by the Muslims, to convert to Islam. If that happens to a respected pastor, just imagine the condition of common Christians who have to mingle with the Muslims in the public sphere. Many have been forced to convert, and the process of making all of Pakistan an Islamic country is in full force.

No Christian speaks nor should speak against the

Prophet of Islam and the Quran. I meet Christians every day. Even though no Christian speaks against the Quran or the Islamic Prophet, we are being accused falsely.

Intention of writing this book

The purpose of this book is not to hurt or insult any Prophet, book, religion, or country. The intention behind this book is *not* to write against the Prophet of Islam or their book. I am a follower of Jesus Christ. Jesus Christ has never taught or preached to speak against any religion, and it is my conviction that by writing or speaking against any religion or book, we do not glorify God. It is also not my aim to write against the government of Pakistan. The intention behind this book is to let the world know how Pakistani Christians are facing challenges and paying a price to be a Christian.

I wanted to do something for my Christian brothers and sisters, to be a voice for those who are voiceless in Pakistan. I know what it means to be a Christian living in Pakistan. This book was actually inspired by my friend, G.W., who encouraged me to write about the everyday life of a Pakistani Christian. He told me the world does not know how severe the suffering and persecution is in Pakistan. I have personally experienced that many people do not think there are Christians in Pakistan.

This book is a mission in itself, and I do pray that it can help people to understand the challenges and sufferings of Pakistani Christians. It is the cry and the tears of every Pakistani Christian that I am trying to compile in a book. I salute all Pakistani Christians, especially those who have been martyred in the name of Jesus Christ, those who are injured, and those who are in jail, not because they have committed any crime, but because they believe in Jesus Christ and are Christians in the Islamic Republic of Pakistan.

I want to stress that this book is not the work of my own imagination but is a compilation of news articles of incidents that have taken place in Pakistan from the time of the installation of the blasphemy law, 295-BC. I am an eyewitness of the majority of the incidents. Most of the pages in this book are taken from different online sources and are not my own words. The sources are given credit where possible, but many of the credits are missing due to the loss of data. I want to thank all of the resourceful websites and media for making this book possible.

The intent of this book is to inform the rest of the world, especially the Christian world, about what is happening in Pakistan because of the very dangerous blasphemy law, 295-BC.

PART 1

The Persecution of Christians

The persecutions of Christians can be truly followed from the primary century of the Christian period to the present day. Early Christians were abused for their confidence because of both the Jews from whose religion Christianity emerged and the Romans who controlled a considerable number of the grounds lands over which early Christianity spread. Right off the bat in the fourth century, Christianity was legitimized by the Edict of Milan, and it in the end turned into the State church of the Roman Empire.

Christian evangelists, just as converts to Christianity, have been the target of persecution as far back as the development of Christianity, occasionally to the point of being martyred for their faith.

The splits of the medieval times and particularly the

Protestant Reformation some of the time incited serious clashes between Christian groups to the point of mistreating one another.

In the twentieth century, Christians were oppressed by different governments including the Islamic Ottoman Empire as the Armenian Genocide, the Assyrian Genocide and the Greek Genocide, just as by agnostic states, for example, the Soviet Union, Communist Albania, and North Korea.

CURRENT SITUATION (1989 to present)

Persecution of Christians in the modern era

According to Pope Emeritus Benedict XVI, Christians are the most persecuted group in the contemporary world. The Holy See has reported that over 100,000 Christians are violently killed annually because of some relation to their faith. According to the World Evangelical Alliance, over 200 million Christians are denied fundamental human rights solely because of their faith. Of the 100-200 million Christians alleged to be under assault, the majority are persecuted in Muslim-dominated nations. Paul Vallely has said that Christians suffer numerically more than any other faith group or any group without faith in the world. Of the world's three largest religions Christians are, allegedly, the most persecuted with 80% of all acts of religious discrimination being directed at Christians who only make up 33% of the world's population.

PART 1: The Persecution of Christians

Every year, the Christian non-profit organization Open Doors publishes the World Watch List, a list of the top 50 countries that it designates as the most dangerous for Christians. The 2018 World Watch List has the following countries as its top ten: North Korea, Afghanistan, Somalia, Sudan, Pakistan, Eritrea, Libya, Iraq, Yemen, and Iran.

In the Muslim world

Muslim countries are where the death penalty for the crime of apostasy is in force or has been proposed as of 2013. Many other Muslim countries impose a prison term for apostasy or prosecute it under blasphemy or other laws.

Christians have faced increasing levels of persecution in the Muslim world. Muslim-majority nations in which Christian populations have suffered acute discrimination, persecution, repression, violence, and in some cases death, mass murder, or ethnic cleansing include: Iraq, Iran, Syria, Pakistan, Afghanistan, Saudi Arabia, Yemen, Somalia, Qatar, Kuwait, Indonesia, Malaysia, the Maldives.

Furthermore, any Muslim person—including any person born into a Muslim family or any person who became a Muslim at a given point in his or her life—who converts to Christianity or re-converts to it, is considered an apostate. Apostasy, the conscious abandonment of Islam by a Muslim in word or deed, including conversion to Christianity, is punishable as a crime under applications of the Sharia. There are, however, cases in which a Muslim will adopt the Christian faith secretly without declaring his/her apostasy. As a result, they are practising Christians, but they are still legally Muslims, and they can face the death penalty according to the Sharia. Meriam Ibrahim, a Sudanese woman, was sentenced to death for apostasy in 2014 because the government of Sudan classified her as a Muslim, even though she was raised as a Christian.

A report by the international Catholic charity organization Aid to the Church in Need said that the religiously motivated ethnic cleansing of Christians is so severe that they are set to disappear completely from parts of the Middle-East within a decade.

A report commissioned by the British foreign secretary Jeremy Hunt and published in May 2019 stated that the level and nature of persecution of Christians in the Middle East "is arguably coming close to meeting the international definition of genocide, according to that adopted by the UN." The report cited Algeria, Egypt, Iran, Iraq, Syria, and Saudi Arabia where "the situation of Christians and other minorities has reached an alarming stage." The report attributed the sources of persecution to both extremist groups and the failure of state institutions.

Muslim nations where capital punishment for the wrong doing of apostasy is in law or has been proposed starting at 2013. Numerous other Muslim nations force a jail term for abandonment or accuse it under profanity or other different laws.

Christians have confronted expanding levels of abuse in the Muslim world. Muslim-dominated countries in which Christian people have endured intense separation, oppression, constraint, viciousness, and now and again demise, mass homicide, or ethnic purifying incorporates: Iraq, Iran, Syria, Pakistan, Afghanistan, Saudi Arabia, Yemen, Somalia, Qatar, Kuwait, Indonesia, Malaysia, the Maldives.

Besides any Muslim individual, including any individual naturally introduced to a Muslim family or any individual who turned into a Muslim at a given point in their life, who changes over to Christianity or re-changes over to it is viewed as a backslider. Apostasy, the conscious abandonment of Islam by a Muslim in word or deed, including changing to Christianity, is culpable as a wrongdoing under utilizations of the Sharia. There are, nevertheless, cases in which a Muslim will receive the Christian faith, covertly without proclaiming his/her renunciation. Therefore, they are practicing Christians, however they are still lawfully Muslims, and they can face capital punishment as per the Sharia. Meriam Ibrahim, a Sudanese woman, was condemned to death for dereliction in 2014 because the administration of Sudan grouped her as a Muslim, despite the fact that she was raised as a Christian.

A report by the worldwide Catholic philanthropy association, Aid to the Church in Need, said that the religiously provoked ethnic exclusion of Christians is extreme to such an extent that they are set to vanish totally from parts of the Middle-East inside 10 years.

A report dispatched by the British outside Secretary, Jeremy Hunt, and distributed in May 2019 expressed that the level and nature of abuse of Christians in the Middle East "is seemingly verging on gathering the universal meaning of massacre, as per that received by the UN." The report referred to Algeria, Egypt, Iran, Iraq, Syria, and Saudi Arabia where "the circumstance of Christians and different minorities has arrived at a disturbing stage." The report ascribed the wellsprings of mistreatment to both fanatic gatherings and the disappointment of state foundations.

In Pakistan, 1.5% of the population is Christian

Pakistani law commands that "blasphemies" of the Qur'an are to be accountable with punishment. At least twelve Christians have been given capital punishments, and about six killed subsequent to being blamed for disregarding blasphemy laws. In 2005, 80 Christians were in a correctional facility because of this law. The Pakistani-American writer Farahnaz Ispahani has called treatment of Christians in Pakistan "drip drip massacre." We will have point-by-point incidents about the blasphemy law in Pakistan and individuals who are charged under law in coming sections, yet here are some of instances of abuses, which have come into light. There are a large number of incidents of the casualties of such mistreatments under blasphemy law, which does not turn out in the light and simply vanish in obscurity on the back streets of Pakistan.

- Ayub Masih, a Christian, was indicted for blasphemy and condemned to death in 1998. He was blamed by a neighbor for expressing that he bolstered British essayist, Salman Rushdie, writer of *The Satanic*

Verses. Lower appeal courts maintained the conviction. In any case, under the steady gaze of the Pakistan Supreme Court, his attorney had the option to demonstrate that the informer had utilized the conviction to compel Masih's family off their land and after that obtained control of the property. Masih has been discharged.[1]

- In October 2001, shooters on motorcycles opened flame on a Protestant gathering in the Punjab, murdering 18 individuals. The identities of the shooters are obscure. Authorities figure they may be a restricted Islamic group.[2]

- In March 2002, five individuals were slaughtered in an assault on a congregation in Islamabad, including an American schoolchild and her mom.[3]

- In August 2002, covered shooters raged a Christian missionary school for foreigners in Islamabad; six individuals were slaughtered and three injured. None of those executed were offspring of foreign evangelists.[4]

- In August 2002, explosives were tossed at a congregation on the grounds of a Christian medical clinic in northwest Pakistan, close to Islamabad, slaughtering three attendants.

---

[1] https://www.europarl.europa.eu/sides/getDoc.do?pubRef=-//EP//TEXT+WQ+E-1998-2021+0+DOC+XML+V0//EN

[2] http://news.bbc.co.uk/onthisday/hi/dates/stories/october/28/newsid_2478000/2478093.stm

[3] https://www.telegraph.co.uk/news/worldnews/asia/pakistan/1388121/Five-killed-as-grenades-are-thrown-into-church.html   (18 March 2002)

[4] http://news.bbc.co.uk/2/hi/south_asia/2173184.stm   (5 August 2002)

- On 25 September 2002, two fear-based oppressors entered the "Harmony and Justice Institute," Karachi, where they isolated Muslims from the Christians and afterward killed seven Christians by shooting them in the head. The majority of the unfortunate casualties were Pakistani Christians. Karachi police Chief Tariq Jamil said the exploited people had their options limited and their mouths had been secured with tape.

- In December 2002, three little youngsters were killed when a hand explosive was tossed into a congregation close to Lahore on Christmas Day.

- In November 2005, 3,000 Muslims assaulted Christians in Sangla Hill in Pakistan and decimated Roman Catholic, Salvation Army, and United Presbyterian churches. The assault was over charges of infringement of blasphemy laws by a Pakistani Christian named Yousaf Masih. The assaults were criticized by some political groups in Pakistan. In any case, Pakistani Christians have communicated disappointment that they have not gotten justice. Samson Dilawar, a priest in Sangla Hill, said the police have not focused on lawful abduction of any of those captured for launching the strikes, and the Pakistani government did not inform the Christians about the ongoing legal procedures toward those culprits.[5]

- On 5 June 2006, a Pakistani Christian, Nasir Ashraf, was attacked for the "transgression" of utilizing open drinking water offices close to Lahore. Christians are

---

[5] http://www.asianews.it/news-en/Sangla-Hill-tragedy:-victims-speak-out-a-year-later-7748.html

considered from the lower tier of the society, and they are considered as untouchables by the mainstream Muslims, and drinking from same tap of water is comparable to the Jews and Samaritans during the time of Jesus.

- One year later, in August 2007, a Christian evangelist couple, Rev. Arif and Kathleen Khan, were gunned somewhere in Islamabad. Pakistani police accepted that the homicides were carried out by an individual from Khan's parish over supposed inappropriate behavior by Khan. This allegation is questioned by Khan's family just as by Pakistani Christians.

- In August 2009, six Christians, including four women and a kid, were scorched alive by Muslim activists, and a congregation was set on fire in Gojra, Pakistan, when savagery broke out after supposed defilation of a Qur'an in a wedding service by Christians.

- On 27 March 2016, a suicide bomber from a Pakistani Taliban group killed in any event 60 individuals and wounded 300 others in an assault at Gulshan-e-Iqbal Park in Lahore, Pakistan. Lahore, Pakistan, and the group who claimed responsibility for the attack, stated it intentionally targeted Christians celebrating Easter Sunday. My older brother and family were also in that park, they shared how Christian brothers and sisters were martyred by the terrorists. It is just nearby their house. In 2016, Easter turned into a mourning day for Christians in Pakistan.[6]

---

[6] https://www.bbc.com/news/world-asia-35909677

- On September 22, 2006, a Pakistani Christian named Shahid Masih was captured and imprisoned for purportedly disregarding Islamic "blasphemy laws" in the nation of Pakistan. He is at present held in imprisonment and has communicated dread of responses by Islamic fundamentalists.

- In August 2012, Rimsha Masih, a Christian young girl, apparently 11 or 14 years of age, and an ignorant with mental handicap was blamed for blasphemy for consuming pages from a book containing Quranic refrains. The claim originated from a Muslim cleric who himself has thereafter been blamed by the police for blaming the young girl. The young girl, and later the Muslim cleric, were both detained and discharged on bail.

- On 9 August 2002 shooters tossed grenades into a church on the grounds of the Taxila Christian Hospital in northern Punjab 15 miles west of Islamabad, executing four, including two medical attendants and a paramedic, and injuring 25 people. On September 25, 2002, unidentified Muslim shooters shot dead six individuals at a Christian charity in Karachi's focal business area. They entered the third-floor workplaces of the Institute for Peace and Justice (IPJ) and shot their unfortunate casualties in the head. The majority of the exploited people were Pakistani Christians.

- On 25 December 2002, a few days after an Islamic priest called for Muslims to kill Christians, two burqa-clad Muslim shooters hurled a grenade into a Presbyterian church during a Christian message in Chianwala in East Pakistan, killing three young ladies. (The individual who was fatally harmed and lost his eye is my companion and neighbor. After this episode, his family moved to city since they were undermined by the neighborhood Muslim group. That individual is a teacher. It is absurdity that if Christians lose their lives, rather than feelings of pity from neighborhood individuals, they need to leave town to spare their families' lives.)

- In February 2006, churches and Christian schools were focused in dissents over printing of the Jyllands-Posten cartoon in Denmark, leaving two old women harmed and numerous homes and much property annihilated. A portion of the hordes was halted by police, yet not all.

- On June 5, 2006, a Pakistani Christian stonemason named Nasir Ashraf was working close to Lahore when he drank water from an open water tap in the office. He was promptly struck by Muslims for "contaminating the glass." A crowd assembled and beat Ashraf, calling him a "Christian dog." Onlookers empowered the beating, saying it was a decent act, which would enable the aggressors to get into heaven. Ashraf was hospitalized.

- In August 2006, a congregation and Christian homes were assaulted in a town outside of Lahore in a land dispute. Three Christians were genuinely harmed and one announced missing after around 35 Muslims consumed structures, defiled Bibles, and assaulted Christians. Based, to some extent, on such episodes, Pakistan was suggested by the U.S. Commission on

International Religious Freedom (USCIRF) in May 2006 to be assigned as a "Nation of Particular Concern" (CPC) by the Department of State.

- In July 2008, a mob stormed a Protestant church during a prayer service on the outskirts of Pakistan's largest city, Karachi, denouncing the Christians as "infidels" and injuring several, including a pastor.

- At least 20 individuals, including police authorities, were injured as 500 Muslim demonstrators assaulted the Christian people group in Gujranwala city on 29 April 2011. (During this episode of mistreatment police was securing Christians for two months. One night, I got a call from a companion informing me that today around evening time, Muslims are going to set fire to the Christian houses, and they got all chemical. [This chemical was same as the ones they effectively attempted in Gojra for burning Christian houses]. That night we safeguarded Christian siblings and took them to safe places and church, and they slept there. That night was intense. The scenes of Christian brothers and sisters running around and migrating from one place to safe place reminded me of the exodus of Israelites from Egypt. I saw the horde next morning was yelling and stoning Christian houses and places of worship.

- During a question and answer session in Karachi, the biggest city of Pakistan, on 30 May 2011, Maulana Abdul Rauf Farooqi and different clerics of Jamiat-Ulema-e-Islam cited "corrupt Biblical stories" and requested to boycott the Bible. Maulana Farooqi stated,

"Our legal advisors are getting ready to request that the court boycott the book."

- On 23 September 2012, a horde of dissidents in Mardan, furious at the counter Islamic film *Innocence of Muslims*, allegedly set ablaze the congregation, St. Paul's secondary school, a library, a PC lab, and homes of four priests, including Bishop Peter Majeed and proceeded to harass Zeeshan Chand, the minister's child.

- On 12 October 2012, Ryan Stanton, a Christian kid of 16 remained in isolation in the wake of being blamed for impiety, and after that, his house was scoured by a group. Stanton expressed that he had been encircled in light of the fact that he had rebuked weights to change over to Islam.

- In March 2013, Muslims assaulted a Christian neighborhood in Lahore, where in excess of 100 houses were scorched after a Christian was affirmed to have made impious comments.

- On 22 September 2013, 75 Christians were murdered in a suicide assault at the notable All Saints Church in the old quarter of the territorial capital, Peshawar.

- On 14 February 2014, Muslims raged the Church building and assaulted school property in Multan. They were driven by Anwar Khushi, a Muslim gangster who hit an arrangement with the nearby individuals' representative. They held onto the Church property, dislodged the individuals, and denied them of their structure.

- On 15 March 2015, two blasts took place at a Roman Catholic Church and a Christ Church during Sunday service at Youhanaabad town of Lahore. At least 15 people were murdered and seventy were injured in the assaults.

- On 17 December 2017, a bomb took nine lives and harmed fifty-seven. The Islamic State of Iraq and the Levant assumed liability.[7] I visited Quetta city and met families and the minister of the congregation. During my visit to families and minister of the congregation after assault on chapel, as a pastor, I asked a question to another pastor. What was the attendance in church after the attack on the next Sunday? The answer was that church was packed, and more people came to church the next Sunday. Instead of losing people, there were more people full of enthusiasm. It blew my mind away. Pastor told me people were so brave and were ready to die for their faith, and nobody can stop them from following Jesus and coming to church. This is the faith that Christians of Pakistan have (Romans 8:35-39). We are proud Christians. We believe Jesus is the son of God and nothing can stop us from following to death (Rev. 2:8-10.)

Then I talked to one family who lost the head of their family and left his widow and kids behind. I had a conversation with the son of the man who lost his life in church while he was worshiping with

---

[7] https://www.nytimes.com/2017/12/17/world/asia/pakistan-quetta-church-attack.html

his family. The son told me that many people die in accidents and many due to diseases, but our father died for Jesus Christ. Therefore, he is a hero for us. It is a big loss to lose father, but we are proud of our father. He lived for Jesus, and he died for Jesus. This is true about every Pakistani Christian. This is how as Pakistani Christians we live everyday life; we are completely uncertain where and when somebody will enter in church and kill us.

Intense Persecution of Pakistani Christians Continued into the Second Half of 2018.

This portrays a grim picture for the small minority community regarding their religious freedom rights. The most troubling aspect of this continued trend is the institutionalized discrimination and intolerance that is apparent throughout the country's laws and practices.

While the constitution of Pakistan declares that all citizens are equal before the law, the reality tells a different story. Christians continue to beg for protection, dignity, safety, security, and equal rights as citizens of Pakistan.

Over the last six months, Pakistani Christians have endured incidents of social discrimination, land theft, sexual harassment, church attacks, hate mongering, and discrimination in educational institutions. The incidents reported below only represent those independently verified by International Christian Concern (ICC).

- On July 9, 2018, Waheed Masih's family in Sheikhupura was assaulted by a Muslim crowd that brought about wounds and harm to their home. A report that a youth Christian kid had purportedly snatched and changed over a Muslim young girl to Christianity was the inspiration driving the assault on Waheed and his family.

- On July 13, 2018, a gathering of equipped Muslims assaulted a congregation in Faisalabad during a worship service. The aggressors raged into the congregation, causing harm to everyone inside. As per a Christians, the aggressors tried to set the congregation ablaze. However, mediation by police spared the congregation from inflicting a greater damage.

- In August 2018, numerous instances of extreme oppression were accounted for. During that month, four Christians were slaughtered, incorporating Amara Bibi in Sheikhupura on August 7, Mehwish Masih in Hyderabad on August 15, Vicky Masih in Lahore on August 16, and Yousaf Masih in Okara on August 17.

- Three Christian women, who will stay anonymous for security reasons, were assaulted in August 2018. These women were from Silakot, Khanewal, and Wazirabad. Asma, a Christian youngster from Khanewal, was additionally assaulted by three Muslim men. The harm brought about by the assault resulted in removal of her uterus by the specialist. Three other Christian women, who will likewise stay unknown, were persuasively changed over to Islam in Karachi, Sargodha, and Sahiwal.

- Several Christians were seriously beaten and tormented in August 2018. Beenish Paul, a Christian lady from Karachi, was thrown out of a building on August 17. She endured serious spinal damages. Vickram John, a Christian from Karachi, lost an eye when his family was assaulted in their home on August 18.

- On August 1, 2018, Farhan Aziz was blamed for blasphemy in Gujranwala. He fled his town and is currently in hideaways.

- Additionally, a congregation in Kasur was savagely assaulted on August 2. The Christian men, women, and kids inside the structure were beaten by a horde for attempting to safeguard the congregation.

- On September 5, 2018, a youthful Christian man, Faraz Badar, was showered with corrosive in Gujranwala. He passed away in the emergency clinic from the wounds on September 15.

- On September 21, 2018, a gathering of Muslims beat Bashir Masih and his family in Gujar Khan and set their van and the top of their home ablaze in light of the fact that those Muslims did not like having Christians in their neighborhood.

- On September 28, 2018, Yaqoob Bashir, a mentally handicapped Christian man, was condemned to life in jail by the Session Court of Mirpurkhas in Sindh for purportedly submitting blasphemy.

- On October 22, 2018, Sharjeel Masih, a Christian boy studying in fourth grade was embarrassed at Government Boys Primary School in Attock when the school's superintendent questioned him for drinking water from a same water tap that the Muslim understudies utilized.

- On November 7, 2018, Ishrat Saba, a female Christian instructor, was explicitly aggravated by her Muslim superintendent at Government Elementary Middle School in Phool Nagar situated in the Kasur District. She was then undermined by a gathering of Muslims when she submitted a question to the specialists.

- On December 13, 2018, two Christian siblings, Qaisar Ayub and Amoon Ayub, were condemned to death by the District Court in Jehlum. They were initially detained in 2015 for purportedly committing the blasphemy.

- On December 30, 2018, a gathering of individuals endeavored to take land from a congregation property named "Gosha e Aman" (Peace Center) in Lahore. The congregation figured out how to recover their property the following day.

- We can see the instances of discriminatory acts towards the Christians in Pakistan in newspapers and media outlets, too. The lowest and most dangerous as well as dirty works are advertised in papers as the vacancy for the Christians. The government offices as well as other workplace give ads on paper specifically to the Christians derogating them as the ones

PART 1: The Persecution of Christians

who will work the dirty, dangerous and demeaning jobs. The jobs of sweepers and the public toilet cleaners are especially allocated to the Christians.[8]

As seen in the incidents above, Pakistani Christians are suffering at home, church, school, and the workplace. Even children are not immune from the reality of discrimination and physical violence. These are only some of the stories that have been out about the sufferings by Christians throughout Pakistan. The government and authorities in Pakistan must take steps to revise the laws and social standards that permit the persecution of Christians.

There is one other incident about oppression faced by Christians in Pakistan that has been reported in the local newspaper. And the incident is heartbreaking. The following is the excerpt from the online newspaper:

---

[8] These are the excerpts of incidents that harmed the Christians in Pakistan that took place only in 2018. There are innumerable accounts in the past yearswhere the Christians are persecuted here in one way or other. Some of the major incidents are discusses in the following parts. The incidents are taken from different online sources and all of them are the part of citation, however not all the online outlets were remembered as these were recorded in the written form after they were found online. It is my regret to not include all of them here, but I thank them all for bringing out the pain that Christians of Pakistan suffer in their own home turf.

Most of the lists of incidents quoted here are taken from a website: www.persecution.org

A poor Christian family in Pakistan is demanding justice after their teenage daughter was allegedly raped by five Muslims. Maria, 15, was kidnapped from her house in Sheikhupura city of Punjab province on June 9 while her father Jalal Masih was out working as a laborer.

Masih accused local businessman Muhammad Sajid and four other men in a first information report (FIR) filed at a police station.

"The locals saw them abducting her at gunpoint in a vehicle. I reached his [Sajid's] office but he was absent. We made contact the next day and he threatened to return her dead body if we informed the police," Masih said in the FIR filed six days after the incident.

"Sajid escaped after leaving Maria on our doorstep on June 10 night. She was extremely scared."

Christian activists are demanding the arrest of the culprits as the news spreads on social media.

According to Legal Evangelical Association Development (LEAD), a non-profit advocacy group providing legal aid to persecuted minorities, 28 Christian girls became victims of abduction, torture, sexual harassment, rape, forced conversion and forced marriages in Pakistan from November 2018 to June 2019.
"The number of unreported cases will be higher as the families of victims usually avoid getting help from biased police officials who support cruel and influential culprits. Only Christian and Hindu girls are victims in such cases. Crimes

against religious minorities are increasing at a high scale in Pakistan," LEAD national director Sardar Mushtaq Gill told ucanews.com.

Interfaith group Rwadari Tehreek launched an anti-rape campaign with a protest on June 15 in front of the Punjab Assembly in Lahore.

"It is a sad reality that dozens of male and female children are subjected to sexual abuse and violence almost every day," said Chairman Samson Salamat.

"Unfortunately, governments and concerned authorities have turned a blind eye toward these serious violations of human rights and the victims are being denied justice because of the lacunas in the justice system."

Salamat called on authorities to organize awareness sessions to sensitize police officials on this important issue.

"Most cases are dealt with in a wrong manner because of the bad treatment and attitude in police stations. The victims only become more victimized. Safe and fully equipped rehabilitation centers should be established for the victims of rape and child sexual abuse," he said.[9]

---

[9] The full story can be found at: https://www.ucanews.com/news/muslims-accused-of-raping-christian-teenager-in-pakistan/85441

Christianity in Pakistan

Christians make up one of the two largest (non-Muslim) religious minorities in Pakistan, along with Hindus. The total number of Christians in Pakistan was estimated at 2.5 million in 2005, or 1.6% of the population. Of these, approximately half are Catholic and the other half Protestant. A small number of Eastern Orthodox Christians are also living in Pakistan, but even we Christian believe that this number, which has been estimated, is not correct and our population is more than that. I must say the Christian population has never been told exactly.

How Christianity Came to Pakistan

According to the records found in the Christian history of Pakistan, Rev. Thomas Valpy French was appointed the first Anglican Bishop of Lahore in 1877 by Westminster Abbey church. He overlooked a large diocese that included all of the Punjab, which was then under British colonial rule, and remained so until 1887. During this period, he also opened the Divinity College, Lahore in 1870. Rev Thomas Patrick Hughes served as a Church Missionary Society missionary at Peshawar (1864–84), became an oriental scholar, and compiled a *'Dictionary of Islam'* (1885). This event is one of the oldest records that is available for the scholars to study about the coming of first Christianity to Pakistan.

Before the arrival of Reverend Thomas records of missionaries who accompanied colonizing forces from Portugal, France, and Great Britain can be traced. Besides

Jesuit, missionaries sent from their Portuguese-held Goa in India built a Catholic church in Lahore, the first in Punjab, around 1597, two years after being granted permission by Emperor Akbar, who had called them to his court in FatehpurSikri for religious discussions. However, this church was later demolished, perhaps during Aurangzeb times. That is why it played an insignificant role in bringing Christianity to Pakistan. Later on, Christianity was mainly brought by the British rulers of India in the later 18th and 19th century. This is evidenced in cities established by the British, such as the port city of Karachi, where the majestic St. Patrick's Cathedral, one of Pakistan's largest churches, stands, and the churches in the city of Rawalpindi, where the British established a major military cantonment.

Missionaries from Europe were successful in converting some numbers of people to Christianity and some Anglican, Methodist, Lutheran and catholic churches were established in the local areas. Even though the stronghold of Islam population was considerably strong, some native population converted to Christianity and were baptised in Christ. Those Christians from Punjab and Northwestern Pakistan are still considered the pioneer natives of Pakistan in God.

Considerable numbers of Christians, which incorporated the native people, consisted of residents from the British army who resided in the colonial Pakistan and many government officials who were locals also became the part of Christian community at that time. With the help of wealthy native Christians and the European people many charitable establishments like schools, hospitals colleges and churches were planted in Pakistan. Big cities like Karachi, Lahore, Rawalpindi and Peshawar benefited a lot from these charitable establishments. There is a large Catholic Goan community in Karachi, which was, established when Karachi's infrastructure was developed by the British before World War II, and the Irish (who were subjects of the British Empire and formed a large part of the British Army) were an important factor in the establishment of Pakistan's Catholic community.[10]

Pakistan became free from the British rule in 1947. Even after the independence, the Christian community in Pakistan remained active in social activities. Muhammad Ali Jinnah was a rising force in Pakistan politics at that time He was popular among all the faith communities including the Christians. The Christian communities from different parts of Pakistan as Punjab and Sindh openly supported the political philosophy of Jinnah and his party Muslim League. Jinnah's promise of equality to all faith groups in Pakistan motivated the support from Christian community to him. He became the founding figure of Pakistan in its history and he lived according to his promise of equality to all citizens but his successors diverted from the promise and the present day plight of Pakistani Christians began to sprout.

Despite the promise of founder of Pakistan to all the citizens, that they will have equal rights, the country decided to declare itself as Islamic Republic in 1956. Islam

---

[10] http://www.wafpak.org/pages/christianity%20in%20pakistan.html

became the national identity of Pakistan people and the reference to all the Pakistan's laws. After Pakistan declared itself as Islamic country, many conflicts arose between the then heavily populated Hindus and the Muslims. Because of that there was a mass population exchange between Pakistan and India upon which many people, including Christians, fled Pakistan. The overwhelmingly minorities which included Hindus, Sikhs, and Christians immigrate to India during that event, and that is a loss to the Christian communities who remained in Pakistan.

At the present nearly 1.5% of Punjab population are Christians. Despite the meagre population of Christians in Pakistan, they have been successful in contributing in some ways to the society of Pakistan. Some of the notable Christian people who contributed in some ways to Pakistan include Justice A.R. Cornelius, who became the first non-Muslim Chief Justice of Pakistan. Cecil Chaudhry, Peter O'Reilly, and Mervyn L Middlecoat are famous fighter pilots who contributed a lot in the Pakistan army and its defense. Education, Health, law, and businesses in Pakistan are also greatly supported field by many notable Christians. Sports is a craze in Pakistan and cricket stands above all. Many famous cricketers in Pakistan are Christians and Yousuf Yuhanna who is revered cricketers in Pakistan was a Christian by birth. However, he converted to Islam due to various forms of pressures in the later days. In Britain, the bishop emeritus of Rochester, Michael Nazir-Ali, is a Pakistani Christian.

Recently, there was more pressure on Pakistan Christian society as it was reported that Pakistan Electronic Media Regulatory Authority (PEMRA) had banned all of the Christian television stations. PEMRA does not allow landing rights for religious content, allowing airing of Christian messages only on Easter and Christmas. This is another bad news after many, which is a form of discrimination toward the Christian's minority of Pakistan.

Escalation of Conflicts between Christians and Muslims in Pakistan

According to journalist Pamela Constable, in the 1980s and 1990s tensions between Christians and Muslims in Pakistan began to "fester." She attributed that the occupation of soviets in Afghanistan gave rise to the military might of Mohammad Zia ul Haq. Haq later on became the leader of Pakistan and implemented the stricter laws regarding religious practices. This conflict was further fuelled by the pressures coming from the Gulf States, which catalysed the spark that initiated the further division between the Christians and Muslims in Pakistan. After the 9/11 attacks on the US, things grew worse with "many Pakistani Muslims" seeing the American response to the attacks "as a foreign plot to defame their faith."[11]

During the 1990s, many Christians were arrested and persecuted under the blasphemy law. The strict blasphemy law became the achilles heel for Pakistan's Christian community as it can put charge on any Christians under any circumstances if some Christian develop a conflicting relation with Muslim person. The law allows the punishment including death under the charge of blasphemy law and it can attack on any vulnerable Christian person at any time. A Bishop from Faisalabad even killed himself for the protest against the persecution of Christians under the pretext of blasphemy law.

Various forms of attacks on Christian communities including bombing of the churches, rapes and criminal activities targeting the Christian communities in Pakistan have led towards the division of the country and with that the plight of Christians in Pakistan have worsened day by day.

Oppression towards Christians

During the years between the independence of Pakistan and 1970s, Pakistan was relatively secular country and freedom on many aspects of society was still prevalent. In 1971 East Pakistan, aka, Bangladesh decided to become independent country and since that time the lone West Pakistan, aka Pakistan became a culturally one unit. This led to the foundation of Islam Republic and the number of minorities narrowed rapidly.

The rise in power of dictators like Zulfikar Ali Bhutto and Zia ul-Haq, the laws of Pakistan were also stringently shifted towards the Islamic law. The Pakistan

---

[11] https://www.washingtonpost.com/news/worldviews/wp/2016/03/28/the-plight-of-pakistans-christian-minority/

law did not restricted the conversion of religion to any other than Islam however; the circumstances and surrounding environment did not allow those kind of conversions. The conversion towards Christian faith in Pakistan were looked down as a punishable offence and many who like to be Christians were forced to hide their confession to themselves. There was no pardon for the offence and many people who confessed their faith had to be displaced and harassed openly. To add the insult to the wound there are increasing incidents of coerced conversion from Christianity to Islam under the threats, harassment and intimidations.

Constitutionally also Christians and other minorities are differentiated and barred from political and governmental jobs and opportunities. No Christian or minorities are allowed to be holding the highest post of president prime minister or any other justice department and ministerial posts. The federal sharia court, which has the power to decide the outcome of accusations on blasphemy laws, has barred Christians and minorities to hold the post of judge.[12] To add the salt to the insult governments encourages the insulting jobs to be handed over to the people aside the Muslims. The post of sweepers, toilet cleaners and other demeaning jobs with low payments are openly advertised in the government run newspapers and media. The mention of "Christians can apply" is hurtful and demeaning to the Christian community.

---

[12] https://web.archive.org/web/20091110133919/http://www.pakistani.org/pakistan/constitution/part3.ch3.notes.html

Christian street sweepers at work

The above-mentioned constitutional fact is embarrassing and shameful example of discrimination. Christians cannot open the restaurant because if people from Muslim background know that it is a Christian restaurant, nobody would come to the Christian restaurant because Muslims hate Christians. They still call Christians (chora) a bad word just like untouchable. There are almost no successful Christian businesspersons in Pakistan but if one Christian will grow his business, many will try to pull him down. We can find that behind the many blasphemy cases against Christians there is an element of hatred and jealousy toward Christians.

It is very difficult for Muslim community to tolerate a Christian businessperson or a successful Christian in his life. In their view, we Christians are there to serve Muslims and work for them as slaves. No powerful Christian can be seen in politics or government because they have set up system in such a way that nobody can come into power except the Muslims. Sometime I feel pity for Christians in Pakistan because there is no way that they can progress in their own country; there is no hope for them because they are completely rejected, discriminated and voiceless. Nothing has been written in constitution, which can benefit Pakistani Christians and Minorities.

Prime minister of Pakistan stated on the minorties day july 29, 2019 that christians and minoritites have a sense that they don't have stake in pakistan because they have not been provided equal rights. We have not given them protection. After that he announced that we gave rights to sikh by opening Kartarpur corridor but he never mentioned anything regarding Christians. Even minor things like a travel ban to Israel for Pakistanis were not mentioned by the Prime Minister. That is how much Christians are discriminated against in Pakistan and shows the mentality of leadership toward the 2% of their population.

Growing homelessness of Christians

Many of the slum areas in big cities of Pakistan are occupied by the Christians. Since these slums are comprise of lots of lands, the eyes of Capital Development Authority (CDA) fell upon those slum areas. Since they saw the slum population and the land have been occupied by the Christians, they decided to demolish the slum areas. Seeing this inhumane act, the Supreme Court ordered the CDA to stop the act and give a written statement on why they are performing that act. The reply of CDA is overwhelmingly astounding. They replied, "Most of these KatchiAbadies (slums) are under the occupation of the Christian community." "It seems this pace of occupation of land by Christian community may increase. Removal of KatchiAbadies is very urgent to provide better environment to the citizen of Islamabad and to protect the beauty of Islamabad."[13] Various human rights activists condemned the response.

The CDA authorities fear that the overpopulation of Christians in slums can bring about the harm to the city as a whole. The demographic unbalance in the slums could in the end be harmful to the whole population of city, so they think that it is necessary to destroy the slums and the Christian population before it is too late. They also mentioned that the increase in numbers of minorities in the slums my effect the Muslim populations in the coming days. They justify their cruelty under the pretence of protecting the constitution and the people of Pakistan. They plan to occupy the land and build the housing sites.

Forced marriages with Christian girls

In a recent visit of the Prime Minister of Pakistan to the USA, Pakistani American Christian Community held a peace rally in front of the White House in Washington DC. The purpose of this rally was to protest against the increasing trend of forced marriages and forced conversions of Christian and Hindu girls in Pakistan.

---

[13] https://tribune.com.pk/story/1016235/islamabads-christian-slum-dwellers-pray-for-christmas-miracle/

The participants demanded:

1. Immediate action must be taken to prevent the forced marriages and forced conversions of Christians of Pakistan and Hindus girls.
2. Weak minorities must be protected and their equal human rights be assured.
3. Discrimination must be stopped against the religious minorities at all levels.
4. Underage girls and women must be protected against violence.
5. Misuse of blasphemy laws must be assured.
6. Victims of Yohana Abad (attack on two churches in Lahore) church bomb blast, including Aslam Pervaiz Sohtra, must be released.
7. Human rights organizations and journalists must be protected.

I saw a letter on Facebook that was written by the Congress of the United States to President Donald Trump regarding the injustices in Pakistan on July 19, 2019. The portion of letter is as follows:

"This is the case with forced conversions, where young Hindus and Christian girls are kidnapped and forced to convert to Islam. Often, they are then married off to men decades their senior. According to an independent Pakistani Watchdog group, there were around one-thousand cases of forced conversions in Sindh Province in 2018 alone. The actual number is certainly higher. Shockingly, there are no laws in Sindh banning forced conversions. There is a law preventing children from being married without parental permission, but this is largely ignored in cases of forced conversions."

Because there is no law against banning forced conversions, it gives freedom and boldness to abuse Christian girls.

Recently in Shadrah, Lahore, a Christian girl, Maria, was kidnapped and raped by five Muslims. The family was seen crying out for justice, but justice was not being done because one culprit was a police officer. They have threatened the family; if you tried to go against them, they will kill the family. It is not only one incident, it is a series of incidents in Pakistan. In Pakistan, the world does not know about many Asia Bibis who are victimized in every nook and corner.[14]

All these things have made Christian girls vulnerable, and they are not safe in their workplaces at hospitals, schools, and companies. It is easy to force them for marriage or abuse them because they are not able to raise their voice in a society where Christians are treated like slaves. Many Christian girls get married to Muslims just because they do not have any securities against the men who attack or trap to abuse them.

---

[14] https://www.ucanews.com/news/muslims-accused-of-raping-christian-teenager-in-pakistan/85441

Forced Labor and Children

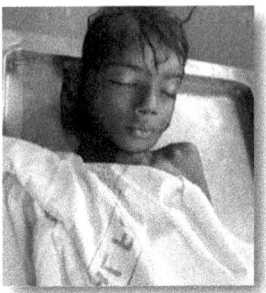

The dead body of Badal Masih who was killed by his boss

An 11-year-old Christian child was killed by his boss over a paltry sum of money in Faisalabad.

The boy named Badal Masih used to work at a place owned by a Muslim boss named Ifran. Being repeatedly mistreated by the owner of the scrapyard Badal made his wish to the owner to leave the job. The boss got agitated and started beating him when he heard that the boy did not want to work for him anymore, and the death occurred through extreme beating. According to the mother of the dead child, the boy was hardworking and did what he was told to do. She added that the life of the boy was taken for no reason.

Asia News reported that the incident took place in the city of Faisalabad and the boss who was responsible for the death is in the hideouts and nobody knows about his whereabouts. Despite being from a poor background, the mother is demanding justice and believes that God will help her to bring the culprit to justice.

The father of the dead child was a drug abuser and did

not work as a breadwinner, so the mother had to work for the family. While he was in the school, Badal felt that he needed to work to support the family, so he started to work in the above-mentioned place. The poverty and the condition of the family forced him to work.

The earnings of the child was about 50-100 rupees per day (30-60 cents). Because of the harsh condition of the house, he borrowed 180 rupees (1.15 USD) to help the family problem. Immediately after the borrowing, the owner began to harass the boy for not returning the money. The boy took the money back from home and returned it to the owner and told that he will no longer work for him. This started the infuriation of the owner and the beating that ultimately led to the death of the child.

Joel Amir Sohotra, a former Christian lawmaker, spoke to AsiaNews about the case. "I strongly condemn this inhuman act of extreme torture and alleged rape of a child," he said.

"This is the sick mindset of a cruel society that does not see minorities and the poor as human beings and so tortures them if they refuse to obey because they think that no one will stand against them over these poor creatures."

"Pedophiles," he believes, "are ruining Pakistan's image in the world. I call upon the government to take stern actions against the culprits and bring them to justice. They must be punished in accordance with the law."

Speaking about Badal, the mother remembers him as "a very obedient child. He wanted to earn something to support the family and me. These cruel owners took his life for no reason."

"My tears can only be wiped away if the culprits are punished harshly and pushed behind bars for the rest of their lives for the sin they committed against my innocent child."[15]

Christian children face different challenges like in schools, too. Here they are discriminated in the classrooms as well. Rauf Klasra, a famous journalist and analyst, in his program on national TV raised the issue that a Christian girl was told by her teacher to leave school because he did not like to teach her. The teacher used to mistreat the Christian girl because of believing in Jesus.

Pakistani school syllabus is Islamic, even subjects such as English are full with Islamite. In the syllabus, it is taught that Jesus is not the Son of God. He was just a prophet, and the Bible is corrupted. Even in Government Schools, all students have to recite Muslim prayer every morning, and I have done this in all my schooling. So many Christian children are forced to make bricks in their whole life as a laborer. They spend their life as a slave.

Brick makers

---

[15] Shafique Khokhar, Asianews.it, 7/12/2019

PART 2

Introduction to Pakistan from Christian Point of View

Meaning of Pakistan has a prehistoric origin and much has been linked to Indus civilization and is Mohenjo-Daro civilization. Before the arrival of Islam to Pakistan in 712 AD, people used to practice idol worship and mostly were Hindu religion. The people were converted to Islam, and ever since, Pakistan still remains one of the stoutest Muslim country in the world. Pakistan was a part of India until 1947 and became independent from India as an Islam state.

a. Christianity History

According to the Church historian Eusebius writing in the 4th century AD, the apostles Thomas and Bartholomew were assigned to Parthia (modern Iran) and India. By the time of the establishment of the Second Persian

Empire (AD 226), there were bishops of the Church of the East in northwest India, Afghanistan, and Baluchistan (including parts of Iran, Afghanistan, and Pakistan), with laymen and clergy alike engaging in missionary activity.

Roman Catholic missionary work took off on the Indian continent with the arrival of the Portuguese in the 16th century. They establishedtheir base in Lahore in 1570. These Portuguese became a stepping-stone for the spiritually deprived people of Pakistan and many became Christians around 16th and 17th century who are considered as the pioneer of Pakistan Christians.[16]

In more modern times, Christianity became firmly established through Protestant missionary work in the late 18th and 19th centuries and has continued to grow ever since. However, due to the strongly increasing pressure in recent years, many Christians have fled abroad to countries like Sri Lanka or Thailand and Malaysia. Since the introduction of the blasphemy laws in 1986, Christians have come under increasing pressure and are victims of roughly a quarter of all blasphemy accusations.[17]

The largest group of Christians belongs to the Church of Pakistan, an umbrella Protestant group consisting

---

[16] https://webcache.googleusercontent.com/search?q=cache:2YRbfwMXJ2EJ:
https://www.opendoors.no/Admin/Public/Download.aspx%3Ffile%3DFiles%
252FFiles%252FNO%252FWWL-2018-dokumenter%252FPakistan-Church-
Facts-and-History.pdf+&cd=1&hl=en&ct=clnk&gl=kr

[17] This has been reported in the world Christian database and is available in
https://worldchristiandatabase.org/

of four major Protestant denominations (Anglican, Methodist, Presbyterian, and Lutheran) and is a member of the Anglican Communion. Other Protestant churches are various brands of Presbyterianism as well as many smaller denominations.

In 1947, the year of the country's independence, the situation for the Christian minority became more complicated as Pakistan officially became a Muslim state. According to the World Christian Database, more than 96% of the population is Muslim, the vast majority being Sunni Muslims. However, there is also a considerable Shiite minority of 10-15%, which suffer persecution as well.

Although the founder of Pakistan said "If we want to make this great State of Pakistan happy and prosperous we should wholly and solely concentrate on the well-being of the people. And especially of the masses and the poor... you are free; you are free to go to your temples mosques or any other place of worship in this state of Pakistan. You may belong to any religion, caste, or creed that has nothing to do with the business of the state..."[18] during the inception of modern Pakistan, we can feel that nowadays the state is not separated from being partial in all the above-mentioned situations. There is no practice by the government in the promise that has been delivered by the founder of the country.

---

[18] http://www.columbia.edu/itc/mealac/pritchett/00islamlinks/txt_jinnah_assembly_1947.html

b. Experiences of Christians in the past

The beginning Christians of Pakistan were not that difficult. Historically the first Christians in Pakistan were not persecuted and they had peaceful life. Socially they were somewhat facing some difficulty but there was no persecution from the state. In the year 1956 the name of Pakistan was changed to Islamic Republic of Pakistan in the constitution then the difficulties for the Christians started and has increased the level of difficulties year by year ever since. In 1979, General Mohamed Zia ul Haq came to power and the Islamic law was forced all over Pakistan. In a way, he used religion to prolong his rule and became popular among religious groups. In addition, the persecution for the followers of other religions besides Islam was intensified and Christians were the main target group for the authorities to hunt down.

Ever since there have been numerous incidents where the Christians were persecuted and faced hardships. We will talk about those incidents in detail below. The difficulties faced by the Christians is found in every strata of the society be it political, economic, and social discriminations.

c. Present hardships faced by faith communities

The Pakistan constitution, political framework, and the all governments are for the most part dictatorial. Religious government is winning in Pakistan. Under this framework, the Christians of Pakistan have neither equivalent political, financial status, nor the equivalent access to accessible open doors in assuming a main job in the national set-up. In spite of the fact that Christians accept and see themselves as top of the line residents of Pakistan, the present political framework accepts the Christians are peasants and are basically at the most minimal level.[19]

The sad fact about being a Christian in Pakistan is that they are constantly reminded at every level that it is not their country. Not being able to claim happily that- I am the citizen of this country proudly- is the saddest fact of life. People without the country are the most hopeless people in the world and Christians in Pakistan are made to feel like that. It is not that Pakistani Christians hate their country, they love their country like any other person but the way that they are treated by the state is a terrifying fact and that is really a subject to ponder upon.

Constitutionally, no Christian has the entitlement to become President, Prime Minister, Chairman of the Senate, or the Speaker of National Assembly (Parliament) of Pakistan. Politically Christians are just the voters and that speaks a volume about their fate in the country. Policymaking needs some representatives in the political arena and this constitutional bar means that there will still be no positive policy towards the Christians in Pakistan. Under the Constitutional bindings, the policies and practices have been adopted by all government and judicial functionaries to ignore and neglect the Christians every time, everywhere at all levels. People at lower level have adopted this as a law that no higher position or rank is given to any Christian.

---

[19] https://www.christiansinpakistan.com/christianity-in-pakistan/

Prior to autonomy of Pakistan, Christian Educational organizations were controlled by Churches yet they were taken over by power and nationalized by the Bhutto government in 1972. Presently, not any more Christian character is being found in these Islamized Christian teaching educational organizations. When Bhutto came to power, a considerable percentage of non-Muslim organizations were denationalized and given to their proprietors however, no Christian establishment was denationalized.

These institutions were the basic centres for learning, social, and cultural gatherings, spiritual development for the Christians. Christian teachers, professors, or students are not seen there. This is the form of persecution; that give rise to the confusion of identity to the believers. Having no place to lean on when in trouble is the worst form of torture one gets. Nobody knows whom to blame for the fate of Christians in Pakistan.

The regime that came into power has saved a few seats for non-Muslims yet it is a cruel reality that these seats are also additionally taken by Muslims. At present, in excess of 5000 government occupations, which were allotted for Christians are currently held by the Muslims. Along these lines, the at least 5000 Christians have been compelled to be jobless and a large number of wards have been denied of their vocation. Forcefully occupying the rights of other is the human right violation from the government but the harsh reality is that there is none to speak out about this.

The number of uneducated and ignorant Christian population have gone up after the nationalization of Christian Educational Institutions and abolishing of the reserved seats for minorities in the government institutions in 1972.. Illiteracy leads to another form of social problem where the minority Christians in Pakistan are forced to be poorer by the bygone time. When a community becomes poorer, there is high chance that the message of gospel cannot be conveyed to other people. The Christians rely on the hope of the future life and prayer but the present life of them is indescribable.

Every government that is formed in Pakistan take out the political statement that favours the non-Muslim minorities from time to time. When foreign dignitaries visit Pakistan, the environment is created in such a way that, there is no problem for the non-Muslim people in Pakistan. When the head of the government visits the western countries, they always put forward the pro-Christian statement but once they return back to Pakistan the situation remains the same. These statements made in the western countries by the Pakistan leaders for the Christians are not practiced in reality. Similarly, the promises that have been delivered in front of the foreign dignitaries also will just remain a promise. There is no change in the socio-economic, political, and religious sector. The government of Pakistan remain rigid to make the world run as it used to.

Constantly a bare and honed Islamic Sword is holding tight the necks of blameless Christians fit as a fiddle of the Law (Blasphemy Laws 295-B and 295-C of Pakistan Penal Code). In the event that any individual disrespects or affronts the Quran, at that point, he must be rebuffed by detainment forever (295-B). And similarly if any individual composes, talks, represents, or does any activity in a disfavoring or offending way, at that point the person in question will need to confront the death penalty, there is no fine or life detainment.[20]

---

[20] Ibid

PART 3

Blasphemy Law and its Effects on Pakistani Christians

The Blasphemy law

According to bbc.com, Pakistan's blasphemy laws carry a potential death sentence for anyone who insults Islam. Critics say they have been used to persecute minority faiths and unfairly target minorities.[21] In order to completely Islamises Pakistan, the military government of General Zia ul Haq added some codes to the existing religious laws. The addition completely boycotts the existence of other religious practice except the Islam.

The previous law ratified by the British rule in India, made it a crime to disturb a religious assembly, trespass on burial grounds, insult religious beliefs or intentionally destroy or defile a place or an object of worship. The maximum punishment under these laws ranges

---

[21] https://www.bbc.com/news/world-asia-48204815

from one year to ten years in jail, with or without a fine.[22] However, this was for the practitioner of all the religions. All the religions were equally punished for the trespassing of the law.

In 1980s, the blasphemy law was created adding some codes to the existing religious laws. The law did not come out at once but various things were added as time passed. Firstly, in 1980 it was passed that making derogatory remarks against Muslims is a punishable offence and one can be jailed up to 3 years. In 1982, another clause was added where willful desecration of Koran was offense that can lead to a life imprisonment. Similarly, in 1986, another clause was added where anything against Prophet Muhammad was a crime punishable by death or life imprisonment. This dangerous blasphemy law in constitution of Pakistan has been the cause of misery of many Christians and people who are supporting the freedom of religion in Pakistan.

It is agreed fact that one's religion is dear to every human individual. Islam is the religion that has been practiced in Pakistan for centuries and people have deep sentiments towards their religion. But, the political leaders that seek power use the religion to fulfil their own wishes. Doing this, they create fanaticism out of religion and the sentiment of people. Blasphemy law in Pakistan is one such example where the sentiments of people and their religious practice have been manipulated by the power hungry politicians to fulfill their selfish motives.

---

[22] Ibid

PART 3: Blasphemy Law and its Effects on Pakistani Christians

If we speak to a faithful Islam, they are always supportive of basic human rights, but the blasphemy law forbids the freedom of human rights and dehumanizes the people of other faiths, specially the Christians. The Muslim brothers and sisters of Pakistan do not care much about the doings of others, but the ones in power always seek opportunity to get limelight, and many have come alive through the way of blasphemy law.

The Bible correctly tells that we are all sinners. We have human nature and we tend to speak and do many things, which we really do not mean to speak or do. If by mistake we say something against Quran or Islam without meaning it in front of some of the opportunists in Pakistan then one might have to face death sentence. Is it a fair law? Nobody can guarantee when or how some words may utter out of a person. Does that qualify for death? No. the blasphemy law is not a law for normal human beings. This is a fact that no Christian speaks against Prophet Islam and Quran. How in a society where 97% of population is Muslim a Christian would dare to speak against their prophet or book, it does not make sense at all. Secondly, this is not teachings of Jesus Christ; nobody glorify Jesus Christ by speaking against Islam. We Pakistani Christian respect others not insult.

We can see in Pakistan if somebody has a personal problem with a person, one has to be very careful. It is very easy to destroy the life of a person using the blasphemy law. Islam is not bad, but the blasphemy law definitely has questionable existence.

We can see some of the examples of people and incidents that has been the result of blasphemy law. The affected people whose life has been destroyed, along with their families, is revolved around one person, Asia Bibi. The fearsome mode of incidents that revolved around the arrest and jail term of Asia Bibi is the focus of this short book. The relevancy of blasphemy law, which caused the death and misery of so many people in Pakistan will be discussed after the study of different people that has been affected by this shocking law.

I. Asia Bibi

Life is beautiful because it is a gift of God. No matter where one lives, one loves their life dearly. Some have comfort of so many privileges while unfortunately many around the world are suffering because of many factors. Societies that have abolished the unequal biases based on the caste, religion, jobs, and families, are able to provide their people with the freedom to choose and live their life according to their choice. However, the case of Pakistan is completely different from other societies.

In many of the underdeveloped countries, people don't have the physical development and are leading daily life in difficult situations. When we take the example of south Asian countries, life is difficult due to poverty, lack of proper infrastructures and the corrupt government, but most of the country can breathe a life of freedom. There is practice of caste system in many societies, but that is bearable in comparison to the state of Pakistan.

Asia Bibi was the victim of all the difficulties in life. Firstly, she was poor; secondly, she was considered un-

PART 3: Blasphemy Law and its Effects on Pakistani Christians

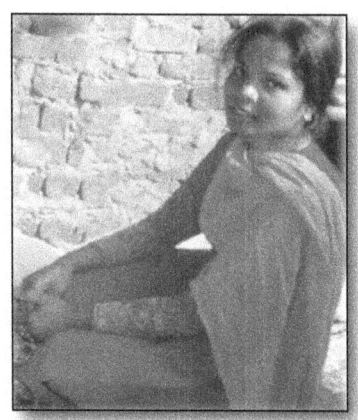

Asia Bibi

touchable because she was Christian; and thirdly, she was female in an Islamic country. She had to work day-to-day job to feed her families.

In one such occasion, she was working in an orchard picking up the fruit in scorching heat. She was a normal human being but being Christian in Pakistani society was her fault. She used to work with people or women of Muslim faith. During the work, the discrimination against her was waged due to a small incident of her drinking water that she fetched before giving it to the other workers. She was scolded and demeaned and was told that she was impure because she was non-Muslim. One thing led to others and heavy discussion between took place. Maybe she spoke few bad words against Islam because she was normal human and everybody is angered when they are demeaned. The incident ended in sour note amongst the participants.

After a few days, she was attacked by the mob, and police arrested her under the blasphemy law. She was jailed

The well from where Bibi collected water

and sentenced for death according to blasphemy law. But, continuous appeal and pressure from different personalities like the governor of Punjab she was not sentenced

Protest against the release of Asia Bibi in Pakistan

to death yet. Finally, after nine years of waiting, she was announced not guilty of charge against the Quran and Prophet Islam by the Pakistan court due to the lack of evidence.

The story does not end here. Violent protests erupted from the senseless group of politicians, and there were three days of unrest in most parts of Pakistan. The government could do nothing but be a spectator in such protests. The government came to its knees and decided to delay the release of Asia Bibi.

Asia Bibi escaped the mob of Pakistan and is said to be safely in third country with her family.

This is one example of the consequence of unforgivable blasphemy law in Pakistan. This incident was opened to society because of the international attention and work of Governor of Punjab. Incidents like this happen in every nook and corner of Pakistan, every day, which does not come out because of fear and negligence of the authorities.

The same story of Asia Bibi is connected to the death of another prominent Pakistani politician named Salman Taseer.

II. Salman Taseer

Salman Taseer was a popular politician from the state of Punjab. While Asia Bibi was in jail and was waiting for the death sentence under the blasphemy law, he was the governor of Punjab. He was born in 1946 in Punjab from a famous poet and an English mother. Before being active in politics, he was a successful businessperson and had invested in many sectors, including telecom and construction companies.

The charges against Asia Bibi were pending, and there was not that much in the news as it was undergoing court process in a local court. However, it became a national issue from a local issue after Taseer put forward a petition to the president for the release of Asia Bibi under the lack of evidence.

Salman Taseer with Asia Bibi

The step taken by Taseer was considered as anti-Islam by the cleric group of Islam, and soon the protest began to come out where mullahs were seeking the death of this anti-Muslim liberal. Not only was be blamed, but in actuality, Taseer was progressive in this issue, and he

PART 3: Blasphemy Law and its Effects on Pakistani Christians

was well known among the Pakistan political circle as critical of blasphemy law. He was vocal in the opposition of the notorious law and wanted to repeal it. It was not a great sight for the Pakistan extremist Islam people.

People started seeking ways to stop Taseer, and the voice of him against the death of Asia Bibi was a perfect opportunity. After he filed a petition to president against the death penalty of Bibi, the mosque began to circulate the fatwa* against Taseer. The continuous brainwashing of the normal people against him became a norm and more and more people were hungry for his life.

One of the political party, Tehereek-e-abbaik, and its leader, Khadim Hussain Rizvicame, came into the limelight after this incident. The leader Rizvi openly sought for the death of Taseer and accused west as third umpire for releasing of Bibi. In a Twitter feed from that time, it can be obtained that he publicly sought for the death of Taseer. According to BBC news, "While preaching, Rizvi would frequently glorify the murder of Salman Taseer."[23]

The cleric declared that the person killing Taseer would be a holy warrior and would be rewarded heavily in heaven. This prompted more people to come forward to perform the act. On January 4th of 2011, he was brought down by his own bodyguard. This is the sad ending of a Muslim who fought against the Muslim law of blasphemy. He saw the evil pertained in the blasphemy law and how the law can bring harm to many normal people. But his sight was not understood by

[23] https://www.bbc.co.uk/news/resources/idt-sh/Asia_Bibi

many people because of which he was killed.

The story does not end here. Malik Mumtaz Hussain Qadri, a young police commando, who Taseer 27 times at point-blank range, became a national hero of Pakistan. The terrorist who killed the prominent politician in Pakistan achieved national attention.

Qadri became a national hero overnight. He was handed over to authority, but he stated that he had no regrets for what he had done. He stated that the punishment for the blasphemy is death. And it was his duty to punish those who go against the Islam.

He was sentenced to death by the court. But his funeral had thousands of people marching on the street. This is the mob justice of Pakistan under the blasphemy law. The resultant outcome of blasphemy law is the country with no justice and human rights. People like Taseer who was in a power position are not spared by this justice. Can we imagine the plight of normal people? This law is outright illegal for the freedom of living.

III. Shahbaz Bhatti

Shahbaz Bhatti was the only Christian with prominence in Pakistan politics. His death was not that surprising as the environment of Pakistan society always dehumanizes the minorities.

Bhatti was born on 9 September of 1968 in Lahore in a

Catholic family. His father was a respected Christian and was a retired army officer.

While he was a student, he was active in school politics, and his focus was the Christianity in Pakistan and the minority groups of Pakistan. He was involved in the association of both the groups and founded one of them, All Pakistan Minority Alliance (APMA). He got opportunity to meet the then president Pervez Musharraf. He later joined the prominent political party in Pakistan, The people's party of Pakistan (PPP). He remained just the dormant member until he became minister for minorities' affairs in 2008.

When he became a high profile politician in Pakistan, he was targeted by many for his past stance and politics in the subject of Christianity and minorities in Pakistan.In November 2 of 2008, a new cabinet was elevated from the lower tier for the minorities' affair in Pakistan and Bhatti became the first federal minister of that ministry. While accepting the position he declared that he was there for the upliftment of minority population in Pakistan who were oppressed and downtrodden by the society. He said that the message of hope, peace, and freedom should be given to the underprivileged society in Pakistan.

After he took the office as federal minister, he did not rest in peace but was always active in support of minorities especially the religious minorities. National campaign for interfaith harmony was launched under his leadership. During his time as federal minister, he took numerous steps in support of religious minorities. These included the launch of a national campaign to promote interfaith harmony, and proposed bill to stop the hate speech and publishing of such materials. He also took bold step to suggest the quota system in government posts for the minorities.

In 2009, Pakistan Christians were attacked in Gojra riot in Punjab. It was a sad incident, and he was the high profile personality with political power to speak for the victim Christians. Since that time, he became the victim of many abuses and death threats from the religious extremists in Pakistan. The threat became more prominent after he spoke for the freedom of Asia Bibi, who was sentenced to death under the blasphemy law.

Because of continuous threats and abuse from all the corners of country, Bhatti felt that his death was near. He even predicted about his death and left a message in case of his premature death. (You can find his message in the YouTube videos if you search them).

The society is made up in such a way in Pakistan that even the person in power would fear for his life if you are a minority person and especially if you are Christian. The blasphemy law is the reason for such a jungle law in Pakistan. To be born as a religiously minority person in Pakistan is to be born with the tag of abuse and threats. Peaceful life is a distant dream for many of the minority's families in Pakistan, and many churchgoers feel that they have been abandoned and left behind by their own state.

The Guardian published a long article about the death of Shahbaz Bhatti: [24]

---

[24] https://www.theguardian.com/world/2011/mar/02/pakistan-minister-shot-dead-islamabad

PART 3: Blasphemy Law and its Effects on Pakistani Christians

Self-described Taliban gunmen have shot dead Pakistan's minorities' minister, Shahbaz Bhatti, an advocate of reform of the country's blasphemy laws, as he left his Islamabad home.

Two assassins sprayed the Christian minister's car with gunfire, striking him at least eight times, before scattering pamphlets that described him as a "Christian infidel". The leaflets were signed "Taliban al-Qaida Punjab".

Bhatti's 22-year-old niece Mariam was first on the scene. "I rushed out to find his body covered with blood. I said "uncle, uncle" and tried to take his pulse. But he was already dead," she said at Bhatti's house, extending a bloodstained palm. The sound of wailing women rose from the next room.

Pakistan's Prime Minister, Yusuf Raza Gilani, consoles relatives of Shahbaz Bhatti Pakistan's Prime Minister, Yusuf Raza Gilani, consoles relatives of Shahbaz Bhatti, the slain minister for minorities.
Photograph: Faisal Mahmood/Reuters

Bhatti's assassination was the second killing of a politician in Islamabad over blasphemy in as many months, following the assassination of the Punjab governor Salmaan Taseer outside a cafe a few miles away on 4 January.

Dismayed human rights activists said it was another sign of rising intolerance at hands of violent extremists. "I am sad and upset but not surprised," said the veteran campaigner Tahira Abdullah outside Bhatti's house. "These people have a long list of targets, and we are all on it. It's not a matter of if, but when."

The only Christian in Pakistan's cabinet, Bhatti had predicted his own death. In a farewell statement recorded four months prior, to be broadcast in the event of his death, he spoke of threats from the Taliban and al-Qaida.

But he vowed not to stop speaking for marginalised Christians and other minorities. "I will die to defend their rights," he said on the tape released to the BBC and al-Jazeera. "These threats and these warnings cannot change my opinions and principles."

Lax security did not help. Witnesses and police said Bhatti was travelling with just his driver when he came under attack less than 50 metres from the Islamabad home he shares with his mother.

A small white car carrying gunmen blocked his way. After an initial burst of fire they dragged Bhatti's driver from the vehicle, then continued firing through a side window. "It lasted about twenty seconds," said a neighbor, Naseem Javed. "When I rushed out, I saw the minister's driver standing by the car, shivering, and his niece weeping and shouting."

"They fired 25 bullets," said a police officer beside a bullet-pocked pavement, holding a handful of brass Kalashnikov bullet cases.

As they left the gunmen flung pamphlets on to the road that blamed President Asif Ali Zardari's government for putting an "infidel Christian" in charge of a committee to review the blasphemy laws. The government insists no such committee exists. "With the blessing of Allah, the mujahideen will send each of you to hell," said the note.

Last November, Bhatti joined Salman Taseer in championing the case of Asia Bibi, a Christian woman who was sentenced to death last November for allegedly committing blasphemy against the prophet Muhammad.

"This law is being misused," Bhatti told *Open* magazine at the time. "Many people are facing death threats and problems. They're in prison and are being killed extra-judicially."

The government later distanced itself from the blasphemy reformists, repeatedly stressing that it had no intention of amending the law, leaving Bhatti and Taseer politically isolated. Now that both men are dead, angry supporters

PART 3: Blasphemy Law and its Effects on Pakistani Christians

> say the government bears some responsibility for not protecting them politically, if not physically.
>
> "The government distanced itself from anyone who took a stand on blasphemy. I blame them for being such chickens," said Abdullah.
>
> Ali Dayan Hasan of Human Rights Watch said Bhatti's death represented "the bitter fruit of appeasement of extremist and militant groups both prior to and after the killing of SalmaanTaseer."
>
> The embattled Christian community also voiced concerns about its safety. "We feel very insecure," said Bhatti's brother in law, Yousaf Nishan. "In this society you can't open your mouth, even if you want to say something good, because you're afraid who you might offend."
>
> The assassination raised fresh questions about the safety of Sherry Rehman, a parliamentarian who also championed reform of the blasphemy laws, and who has been in semi-hiding since January.
>
> She was not available for comment. Friends said she may have gone into hiding again, fearing for her safety.
>
> —*The Guardian, March 2, 2011*

We can see from the article that the death of a prominent politician in Pakistan was executed in very simple manner and not much has been done since then to bring the culprit to justice till today. The blasphemy law victimizes the minorities in Pakistan in easy way.

IV. Shazad and Shama Masih

In another example of brutal abuse of blasphemy law is the sad death of Shazad and Shama Masih, the couple of 28 and 25. They had four children, and Shama was pregnant with 5 months old waiting for birth.

They were the young Christian couple who were firstly beaten, then locked in and burnt alive.

The couple used to work in a brick factory in KotRadh-Kishan, a village a distance from the Lahore city. The owner of the brick factory was a Muslim. In constant nagging and demeaning of the couple for being Christians, they were harassed from time to time. In addition, in once such instance the wife Shama was blamed for burning the pages of Quran while she was burning some old papers that belonged to her father.

Shahzad had some debt to pay to the owner of the factory, but due to his illness, he was not able to work continuously in the brick factory. That prompted the owner to show his power, and they came to the family's house and beat them up. The owner gathered the mob of around 400 people and brought the anarchist justice to the Christian family.

The mob not only beat them, but they locked them inside a small room made from the brick from the same

PART 3: Blasphemy Law and its Effects on Pakistani Christians

The brick factory where the couple worked

factory. As time passed the mob became more and more agitated, and finally they broke inside and set the couple on fire. The unforgivable law in Pakistan was yet again successful to take the life of innocent minority. The fearsome blasphemy law has once again given shelter to the lawless Pakistan. We Christian leaders protested for the justice of the innocent couple's killing, and later some Muslim leaders and Christian leaders invited me to pray in the memorial service of this couple. Most of the culprits have been realised already who burned alive this couple. Nobody knows until when this mob injustice will be continued.

V. The Case of Stephen Masih

Yet in another horrendous case of misuse of blasphemy law, Stephen Masih, a mentally disabled Christian man, was charged with "blasphemy" in Punjab, Pakistan, on 11 March following a complaint by two Muslim men who claimed he "made derogatory remarks against the Holy Prophet Muhammad in their presence" and ignored their requests to stop.

Stephen Masih is a mentally ill, 42-year-old person who lived with his sister and a sick mother. Because he acquired typhoid fever while he was still young at the age of 10, he had damage in some parts of his brain. Because of their poverty, the family could not afford the medication, so he continued to live with the illness till this age. Because of his illness, he cannot control the outbursts from his mouth while in groups, and the foul language that he used to speak is uncontrollable.

On one such day, he was alone in home while his sister went to church, and he got involved in a verbal fight with the wife of a neighbor, and it got ugly. The woman threatened him that they will launch a complaint against him with the police as he frequently used foul language against the woman. The complaint, which carries a mandatory death penalty, was launched against him, and he is in custody in Sialkot district.

Before taken into custody, Stephen was brutally beaten under the leadership of local Muslim clerics. The beating did not stop even after the continuous begging of his sister and the people who had the knowledge of his illness. The sister agreed that her brother was in the habit of using bad language because of his illness, and after living in that neighbourhood for more than three decades, she felt that her family is under danger from the mob justice under the pretence of blasphemy law.[25]

---

[25] https://barnabasfund.org/en/news/mentally-disabled-christian-man-charged-with-blasphemy-in-pakistan

Any person or a group of people can destroy the life of a Christian family under the use of blasphemy law. There is no court; no judge but direct judgment if somebody has some issue against any Christian in Pakistan. The mob will not seek for the reason they just go for attack. The physical condition, the mental condition and other aspects of the accused but they just start their mob justice once they find somebody has accused them. The mob justice has been prevailing for many years in the blasphemy cases. The mob is powerful and they have been doing justice on the roads and taken lives of many Christians on the name of blasphemy. Just one announcement by imam in mosque's loudspeaker is enough to agitate mob, they will kill Christians and burn the houses, and whole Pakistani Christians will be under their judgment.

VI. Attacks on Shantinagar, Khanewal

There was an atrocious mob attack in the Christian village of Shantinagar and the areas around it on the 5th and 6th February of 1997. I consider this attack a result of the awful blasphemy law. The destruction caused by the mob attack was so horrendous that people of the locality cannot remember such destruction in long history. Bishop John Joseph who fought whole his life against this law once stated that "Ironically, it is the mistake of law, which happens to be the first cause behind such incidents."[26] He was right from the first moment that this law is not for peace but for division

---

[26] A Peaceful Struggle, Ed. Fr. Khalid Rashid ASI. Box 87, G.P.O., Bishop's House, Faisalabad, Pakistan, May 1999, p. 111

and conflicts amongst the pupil of the same country.

Political parties and the politicians turn blind eyes toward such atrocities, which happen to their own constituencies simply because the victims are minorities. They are more interested in the religious group that have majority to vote and their religious sects. In countries that are more democratic, the political leaders look at all the groups of people and try to represent all stratum of society, but in Pakistan, all that a leader seeks is majorities of voters, and because of that, there is no punishment for the mobs that are performed by the majority of people. The culprits, instead of facing the punishments, just roam around freely with their heads held high due to this kind of actions by the people in power.

Due to the loopholes in the blasphemy law, it has been used in wrong ways in many of the incidents that happen in the society frequently. The anger and jealousy that arises during the business and other social platform end up in the wrong use of blasphemy law. The minorities, since they don't have rights to vote for their candidates, just stay aside and let the atrocities happen as if nothing has happened.

Since this law came into mainstream society during the time of dictator Zia ul Haq in 1986, the growing tensions in the society have cracked the country into different factions. Non Muslim minorities have been the target of unnecessary torture, and many have lost their life and livelihood because of this law. The attitude of the ordinary citizens is such that it is taken for granted that non-Muslims must have committed such offenses. One such incident is the mob attack in the village of Shantinagar.

PART 3: Blasphemy Law and its Effects on Pakistani Christians

There was a peaceful village near the city of Khanewal named Shantinagar (Shanti in Pakistan language means peace). The village was established long before the independence in 1916 while Pakistan was still under British rule. During the early days of the gospel in Pakistan, Shantinagar was heavily influenced by the Salvation Army and remained so for a long period of time. As the majority of residents in the village were Christians, it became a different example in Pakistan. The villagers were given the land after the land reform in 1972.

There are estimated 25,000 residents in the village. In addition, the vast amount of fertile land that they own, most of the villagers are well to do despite the high percentage of illiteracy. The villagers were involved in agriculture, raising animals plus fruit and vegetable growing. All in all we can say that the Christians in this village had prospered compared to the Christians in other parts of Pakistan.

Even though the majority of the populations were well to do Christians, they did not look down on their Muslim neighbors. They even considered building a mosque for their Muslim brothers, and they all celebrated with joy when the mosque was inaugurated. There was a perfect example of unity in the divided country. Even after the treacherous attack on the village by the mob, the Christians in the village did not forsake their Muslim neighbors, and they used to share whatever they had with them whenever the Muslim brothers were in need.

The attack on Shantinagar is linked to the recent past incident when police raided a local resident named Baba on the excuse of some people gambling and preparing liquor. As the police did not find any evidences, they started to search the house vigorously and while doing so a Bible from the house fell down on the ground. The officer was little bit agitated, and he kicked the Bible. Not only did he do that, he took Baba into custody and took him to the nearly police station.

When the villagers heard about the incidents, some respected members of the village went to the police station to release Baba who was under custody. But when Baba told the elders about the bible they became irate and demanded the police to register case against those officers involved. A team of police was sent to the village to find out more about the incident and it was proved that the defilement of bible by the officer was true. Despite the proof, the reluctance was found for registering the case against the involved police officers.

The reluctance of police filing a case against their own fellow officers agitated the Christians in Shantinagar and around more and there was a huge protest march. Thousands of Christians marched to the office of commissioner of police and demanded that justice would be done. The pressure was so huge that the deputy commissioner of police assured the Christians that the case will be registered, and the culprits would be suspended.

The case was registered, but there were negotiation from police sides demanding that they take back the case. The villagers did not agree to the demand at which point the commander who was responsible for the negotiation threatened the villagers. The enmity between

PART 3: Blasphemy Law and its Effects on Pakistani Christians

the villagers and police developed during this incident. However, the national newspaper reported that three officers who were involved in village of Shantinagar were suspended. Then it was found out that shortly after the suspension, the three goon police were reinstated in their post. The villagers took it as an insult because the law was not followed by the government.

The incident took a deeper turn when in general election one of three police who were reinstated was assigned to the village of Shantinagar for election duty. This was more insulting to the villagers, and they took the matter to higher officials, which added more fuel to the previous enmity.

The plot was created by the police to take revenge on the villagers. There was an abandoned mosque in the nearby village, and police found some torn pages of Quran and not only that, there were some papers which were filled with words cursing Prophet Muhammad. Police put the blame on one of the villagers from Shantinagar, but the irony was that the man who was charged for writing such words was illiterate.

Immediately, the news traveled like wildfire, and the mosques began to announce on their loudspeakers about the defilement of Quran. The mullahs accused the Christians from the village of Shantinagar for committing blasphemy against Quran and Muhammad. This ignited the fire, and there were protests everywhere in Khanewal and surrounding areas. The Islam religious leaders declared war against the Christians. Three Christians from the village of Shantinagar were arrested, and this hap-

Village of Shantinagar after attack

pened within half an hour of the case filed by the person who found pages in the abandoned mosque. They were kept in an unknown place. The arrest of three people did not end the protest, but it was prolonged by mob attacks in Shantinagar, and it was done under the noses of police.

The attack resulted in destruction of churches, Christian houses, shops and the confiscation of valuable goods. Some of the looters who were arrested later on involved local religious leaders, village heads, and even some police officers and some of the looted materials were confiscated from them as evidence. The reports that came afterwards stated that 118 cattle and valuables worth thousands of rupees were handed over back to owners and the team of magistrate are still in search of other looted materials in nearly villages.

The report also found out that 80% of the village of Shantinagar was damaged and some 800 homes that belonged to Christians were devastated. The destruction also included thirteen churches, four community buildings, two chemist shops, two schools, fifteen shops two boys' hostels, and about two thousand bibles. Reports suggested that despite the complaint for the loss of those properties the government has done little or nothing to compensate the loss and property. There have been some joint efforts of Muslim and Christian humanitarian acts to support the village of shantinagar nothing more have been done or promised from the side of the government.[27]

Despite the open vandalism and destruction of a peaceful village, not much has been done for the sake of those who have been attacked by the mob. As mentioned previously, the political representatives of the local areas work for the religious groups, and they cannot raise voice against such attacks on the minorities. The selfish motives of the political leaders do not look at the interests of minorities, and such mob attacks under the blasphemy law have always won the case in Pakistan.

VII. Church Bombings

The blasphemy law has caused numerous attacks in Pakistan, and they range from minor threats to the bombing of the churches. We hear the news from time to time about the bombings of churches by the unknown groups, and it is very easy to justify those bombings under the blasphemy law. Listed below are the incidents of attacks in different parts of Pakistan at different

---

[27] https://www.pakistanchristianpost.com/opinion-details/3315

times. All these condemnable offenses are caused due to the existence of blasphemy law.

1. Attack on Methodist church in Quetta in December of 2017

The attack occurred in a Methodist church in the city of Quetta near the border of Afghanistan. The attack left nine people dead and more than 50 injured, including women and children. The church was packed with worshippers on Sunday morning, and four gunmen, including a suicide bomber, stormed into the church compound.

The church compound after the attack

Two suicide bombers were stopped by the police, but one of the bombers exploded the bomb resulting in the casualties. The other bomber was stopped by the armed force. Two of the attackers on the church were able to flee the scene of the incident. It is sad that Pakistan churches have to put security guards in the church due to such incidents. I have visited and seen how bombers entered, and one guy tried to stop them by closing the gate, but they jumped the door and entered and shot the guy who I have personally met. He is alive but his one side is paralyzed. I saw the sanctuary was damaged when a bomber blasted himself outside the sanctuary gate and did not find a way to enter into the sanctuary because the worshipers closed the door from inside. The sad fact is that they were looking from the inside at what the bombers outside were doing, but they had no weapon to protect themselves. If bombers had entered into the sanctuary, damage could have been so big.[28]

2. Attack on Easter celebration

On 16th of March 2016, many Pakistan Christians were celebrating Christmas in a public park in Lahore. The after scene of the attacked place was heart wrecking. Parents were searching for their children and children searching for parents amongst the piles and heaps of corpses

Scenes of aftermath of attack in the public park in Lahore

---

[28] https://www.bbc.com/news/world-asia-42383436

were not human at all. The extent that a human can go after another human is not fathomable, and the scene seen here was imaginable only in the apocalypse movies.

All together, 70 people lost their life in this inhumane act, and nearly 300 people were injured, some in very serious ways. We cannot imagine the mental health of those people who were attacked, as they cannot forget this horror in their entire life.

A faction of a Talaban-related group claimed responsibility for their cowardly attack. This was one of the deadliest attacks in the history of Pakistan Christianity. The reason behind the attack was not clear, but many connected this incident to the death sentence given to Qadri, who killed governor of Punjab, Salman Taseer. That case was related to the blasphemy law, so these casualties in Lahore can be connected to the result of blasphemy law.29

3. Bomb blast in two churches in Lahore

In March of 2015, two bombs were blasted in two different churches of Lahore. The churches were located in the crowded city area, hence the attack was planned for the maximum damage of the people and property. Fourteen people were dead and many more injured in this terror act. Another faction of Taliban claimed the responsibility of the attack with pride. I have met the families and pastor. It was heartbreaking to hear that one woman lost her son and son-in-law in church during this attack. One young boy, Akash, who was providing secu-

---

[29] https://www.bbc.com/news/world-asia-35909677

PART 3: Blasphemy Law and its Effects on Pakistani Christians

rity voluntarily tried to stop the bomber, but he blasted himself outside the church wall. The complete Christian community was terrified after this attack in Yohana Abad, the biggest Christian community in Pakistan.

4. Attack in historic All Saints Church in Peshawar.

In 2013, one of the biggest attacks to the Christian community took place where two suicide bombers blew themselves up in a historical church of Peshawar called All Saints Church. The attack left 75 people dead and more than 300 injured. The attack took place after the Sunday worship service, and the people were coming out of the church area. This caused the maximum casualties.

Scene of protests by the Christians in Pakistan after the Peshawar incident

The two bombers simultaneously blew themselves up. The witness says that the second bomb had more sound then the first and later on it was found that in order to take the maximum lives, the suicide bombers had added extra materials on their bodies. I have visited this church after the attack; it is located in the main market of Peshwar city. This attack was so severe that the place where the bomber blasted himself there became a pit on the floor and his head was found from the neighboring house. I saw reporters crying who were giving coverage to this incident.

The attack gave rise to many sympathizers. The political leaders were all using the same words of sympathy, but not much has been done since then to minimize such attacks in Pakistan. These incidents angered many in Pakistan, and the Christian community was very much agitated. The Christians from different cities organized the protests in major cities in Pakistan and united many factions of Christians under the same umbrella of Christ. The present Prime Minister of Pakistan, Imran Khan, also condemned the attack and urged the government at that time to act swiftly to end such atrocities.

Even though there were many sympathizers of Christians after this incident, the minor Christians still feel unsafe and vulnerable living in Pakistan, which has the dangerous blasphemy law.

A group of militants claimed responsibility for the bombings. They gave the reason as to retaliate against the drone strike of US in the northern part of Pakistan.

5. Gojra incident

In Gojra town in Punjab nearly 40 Christian houses and church was burned down by the mob in 2009. Eight people were burnt alive. The blame on the Christian community was that they desecrated the Quran. Without going for punishment formally through court and official means, the militants decided to take the matter in their own hands. This is the example of society where justice and human rights are the things of distant cry.

Even the Muslim community in Pakistan were not happy with these incidents. There were many protests amongst the intellectuals regarding this inhumane act and many felt that the act was not according to the teaching of Quran. I would like to take two letters to the editors of the *Dawn*, which is Pakistan's oldest and most-read English newspaper.

> THE extremely despicable riot at Gojra is just another example of blind bigotry that our society has been harbouring against followers of faiths other than ours.
>
> We are ready to kill for the very same religion that we so loudly proclaim to be a peaceful one. There are many ironies attached to this particular incident. For one, the desecration has not been proved.
>
> Did anybody of the zealous Muslim majority of that area, anyone at all, bother to ask for an investigation with proper evidence and supporting proofs of the allegations?
>
> What about four witnesses? Can anyone of that insane mob relate to us a single incident where the Holy Prophet

(PBUH) asked for torching down whole communities even in the case of a proven offence, let alone for totally unfounded allegations? Whatever happened to the Islamic principles of tolerance and justice? Whatever happened to the supposedly equal rights of minorities in a so-called Islamic state?

This is how we behave with minorities in our own country and at the same time bemoan when the rest of the world generalises the actions of the Taliban and Al Qaeda on all Muslims.

This incident also relates to another long forgotten aspect our educational curriculum. The syllabus that is taught in our schools does not teach anything substantial on interfaith harmony. It does not teach its students to respect other religions and their followers.

This is about time that those concerned with the formulation and implementation of school syllabi induct chapters on religious harmony, respect of other religions and tolerance in as stressful a manner as possible. Our syllabus should not be polluting young minds with hatred; it should not impart a sense of Muslims-are-greater-than-thou attitude but should inculcate in young minds the essentials of being responsible, rational, and tolerant citizens.

We, the Pakistani Muslims, apologise to the whole Pakistani Christian community for what happened in Gojra.

A.T.[30]
Via email
https://www.dawn.com/news/867960

---

[30] https://www.dawn.com/news/877158

Another email sent to the editorial board of *Dawn* has similar sentiment in its writing. The letter written discourages taking the law into our own hands.

> PAKISTAN has witnessed another sorry event of intolerance. This time it was Gojra town that remained a battlefield for many hours on August 1. The gruesome arson acts ended with the loss of lives and limbs.
>
> As reported, the main cause behind this act of vandalism was the alleged desecration of the Holy Quran. Undoubtedly, the desecration of the Holy Book is a serious crime, but there is a certain process for trying such acts, which in this case seems to be missing.
>
> We have become a nation with an identity of religious intolerance and extremism, which we claim is against the teachings of Islam. It is a fact that societies are known by their behaviour rather than tall claims.
>
> Peeping into the recent past, one can recall the happening of similar acts. There were detailed reports with overwhelming results. In most cases, personal grudges or issues were the main cause behind the blasphemy allegations. It has been considered a speedy and effective way to level personal scores.
>
> Neither Islam nor our Constitution or local laws allow the public to take the law into their hands. It is the duty of the state to prosecute the matter according to the law and pronounce a punishment if the alleged is found guilty.
>
> The public must never be allowed to resort to acts of arson and vandalism, and the state must compensate the victims of this tragic event by bringing the culprits to book.[31]
>
> A Muslim (Via Email)

[31] Ibid.

These letters to the editor of a prominent newspaper highlight how many Muslims feel about the conditions of Christians and other minority groups in Pakistan. Being a real Muslim does not include one to harm other people based on their faith, but the group of extremist religious zealots have controlled the mind of majority of population of Pakistan, hence the pitiful conditions of law and order.

6. Joseph Colony burning of Christian houses

The incident took place on 9th of March 2013 when Joseph Colony, a Christian neighborhood in Lahore city, was set ablaze by a group of mob. This incident also happened due to the fallacies in the blasphemy law. A total of 173 households, 16 marts, and 2 churches were completely destroyed and left on the ground. The incidents started after two friends Sawan Masih, a Christian, and Shahid Imran, a Muslim, had a quarrel in a petty matter of money. They used to live in different parts of the city but worked in Joseph Colony.

According to the local newspaper, the two got into an arguments when they were drinking together. The argument led to the accusation of Imran to Sawan of blaspheming the prophet Mohammad and Quran. This accusation led to the destruction of the town as a whole. The perfect example of how the blasphemy law can be used to destroy the minorities in Pakistan can be found from this incident.

Even though the local media had the story about the incident, blaming Sawan for his utterance of words

PART 3: Blasphemy Law and its Effects on Pakistani Christians

against Muslim, the investigation by vice reporter found out the different truth about the incident. According to the reporter, Sawan went to Imran's shop to shave. Since he did not have the money at that time, he left without paying and told that he will pay Imran later. After some time, Imran went to Sawan's home to fetch money. Since Sawan was in shower, Imran managed to behave inappropriately with Sawan's wife. Sawan confronted his friend, and this seems to have sparked the flame for the incident.

Imran, being offended by his friend, sought ways to take revenge on his friend. And it was not difficult to do so as the blasphemy law was there to be utilized. He went around mosques and local Muslim neighborhood and started to tell people about how Sawan offended the Muslims. The mob started to get organized, and they started to march toward Joseph Colony. However, they were stopped by the police officers. The mob planned to kill everyone in Joseph Colony and set fire to the houses. According to the vice reporter, even though the police stopped the crowed, they did not disperse the crowd. Instead, they told the locals of Joseph Colony to leave the place or else they will not be responsible for what will happen to them.

Seeing the inflammable situation, the locals of Joseph Colony handed Sawan to the police authorities, but that also did not stop the mob. Thousands of people marched toward the colony, and they were torching the houses down. They used chemicals to burn the houses. They looted the houses and took expensive jewelry with them.

But while in research, the vice reporter found another story related to the incidents. The locals were offered half a million rupees for the plot of land in Joseph Colony by the iron factory nearby the colony. The locals refused the offer, and many suspect that the incident might relate to that. The locals also believe that those iron industries are the main culprit behind the incident, and they firmly believe that Sawan did not commit any blasphemy.[32]

The innocence of the local people as in Joseph Colony is nothing in front of the blasphemy law. There are many cases of misuse of this law to settle the grudges between the people. The law is the strictest form of persecution that minorities face in Pakistan. Anything that is possible to press the minorities can be possible through the loopholes of blasphemy law.

"This country has given us nothing. They destroy our churches, burn our Bibles, yet we cannot do anything. This country doesn't respect us,"[33] told Parveen, 53, another resident who lost everything in the fire to vice reporter.

These few incidents have occurred in the recent past in Pakistan. There are numerous more incidents that have not been reported due to the fear. These examples are the conditions under which the Christians in Pakistan have to live and thrive. With these examples, I would like to take our focus to the organizations that are working for Christians and minorities in Pakistan in the next chapter.

---

[32] https://www.vice.com/gr/article/dp4q5m/blasphemy-laws-in-pakistan-provide-cover-for-all-kinds-of-grudges

[33] Ibid

PART 4

International Humanitarian Organizations Working in Pakistan

There are several human right groups in Pakistan operating for the watch out for human right violations in Pakistan. Human right watch is one of the international organizations that is working in Pakistan. The name suggests that it watches the human right violation in different parts of the world. It has done a good job by reporting the incidents of human right violation. However, that cannot be enough to change the scene of humanitarian crises facing Pakistan.

The activities of human rights organizations and other international organizations are closely monitored by the government and interested parties, and it should be understood that there is a security concern for those workers. Because of that, the full truth about the violation of human rights does not come out of border of Pakistan.

Human rights watch reported that in 2018, at least 17 people remain on death row in Pakistan after being convicted under the draconian blasphemy law, and hundreds await trial. Most of those facing blasphemy allegations are members of religious minorities.

According to the report, blasphemy allegations and related rhetoric from both private actors and officials increased in 2018. However, the government did not amend the law and instead encouraged discriminatory prosecutions and other abuses against vulnerable groups.

The same report stated that in February, Patras Masih, 18, and Sajid Masih, 24, were charged with blasphemy in Lahore. Sajid Masih alleged that the police torture he endured while being held led him to attempt suicide, by jumping out of the interrogation room window. He was badly injured but survived.[34] I visited Sajid in Myo Hospital Lahore along with my team. It was hard to meet him, and police security was very tight around him. Later, I came to know the whole police security personnel is Christian because if the police department had appointed Muslim security men, there were many chances that one of them could kill him. This has been seen already in the case of Salman Taseer (Governor Punjab) and in many incidents. When I saw him, he was just like half dead. His body was swollen, and there were many fractures all over his body. He was unable to speak. Police guys told me you cannot take any photos of him. In fact, they took my phone at the gate before meeting him.

---

[34] https://www.hrw.org/world-report/2019/country-chapters/pakistan

PART 4: International Humanitarian Organizations Working in Pakistan

After a while, Sajid Masih's brother came there. I met his brother and asked him the whole situation, what happened to Sajid, and it was a heartbreaking story. He told me that police guys who were investigating asked Sajid to rape Patras Masih, his cousin who was accused of blasphemy, and Sajid refused and jumped out from six story building. It was so inhumane act that police wanted him to do, but he didn't do this evil act. Patras is still in prison, and one of my friends was with him in jail, and my friend died in jail. The case against Patras Masih was completely based on false accusations.

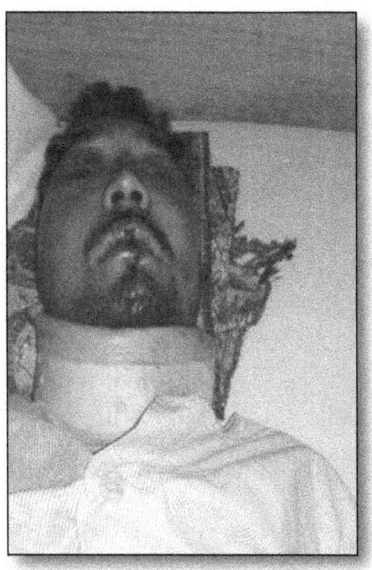

Sajid Masih in Hospital

The humanitarian organizations report the cases and that is done. No actions from the concerned authorities are taken hence the blasphemy law still prevails in the Pakistan justice system.

There are many other organizations in Pakistan that claim to be humanitarian and human rights organizations. However, most organizations are just the spectator of what is going on in the society. When it comes to the persecution of minorities and oppressed, we can find very little work done by them. The organizations who claim to be human rights organizations do not even take out statements when atrocities are forced upon the Christians and minorities of Pakistan.

Many development organizations are also working in Pakistan. However, they are limited to do their jobs in all parts of the country. They have done next to nothing when it comes to the case of oppression of the people by the ones in power.

Faith based organizations in Pakistan

Many faith-based organizations were also working in Pakistan. The Muslim faith-based organizations are highest in number, but despite the low percentage of Christians in Pakistan, the Christian faith-based organizations in Pakistan are in significant numbers. Both the Catholic and Protestant groups have humanitarian organizations under their belt.

The Christian organizations in Pakistan play a prominent role in many sectors, and education is one of the main sectors that have benefited a lot from Christian organizations. Many schools and colleges were established by those organizations. Not only that, but the health sector of Pakistan also benefitted a lot from faith-based Christian organizations.

PART 4: International Humanitarian Organizations Working in Pakistan

The society of Pakistan has benefitted a lot from the Christian organizations, but in recent years those organizations have again been the target of authorities of Pakistan. Ever since the death of Osama Bin Laden in a northern town of Pakistan, it was accused that an international humanitarian organization named Save The Children was collecting information from the local area. Since that time, international organizations were watched carefully, and Christian organizations were most hard hit by the authorities in Pakistan.

According to ChristianToday.com, after the event of the death of Bin Laden, the government revised its legal framework, cancelled registration for all international organizations, and started fresh with 143 applicants in 2015. The process eventually led to the recent appeals and expulsion affecting World Vision and others. Their departure represents a lost opportunity for both socioeconomic growth and human rights progress.[35]

World Vision was one of the biggest international Christian organizations working in Pakistan for more than a decade. In 2018, 27 international organizations were given expulsion orders, but 18 of them, including World Vision, decided to continue working in Pakistan while they appealed the decision. But, later they were given the date of November as the last day that they can operate in Pakistan. The expulsion of World Vision is an example of the unthankful nature of Pakistan, and the work that they were doing was benefitting the needy

---

[35] https://www.christianitytoday.com/news/2018/december/world-vision-out-of-pakistan-international-charities-ngos.html

and poor people, which the government neglects. The step taken by the government made the desperate situations of underprivileged people more desperate and their struggle for health, education and basic necessities have been taken away under the rule of the government. It is unimaginable fact that government cannot do something for people and they are against the ones who is doing something for the sake of those marginalized people.

World Vision began its operation in Pakistan in 2005, focused on emergency relief and development. Over the past few years, the group expanded its programs and "aimed to provide about 800,000 children and youth, directly and indirectly, with access to education, protection, sustainable income generation, health care, food, and better care within their homes and communities."[36] The Christian humanitarian organization, which had 31 staff based in the country, struggled for two years to formally register and went through a nine-month appeals process. Their efforts were funded by a multi-country grant from Canada focused on health and a US grant focused on community building.

"World Vision regrets the effect that the cessation of our work will have on the vulnerable communities with whom we worked, but respects the government's right to decide who may work in the country,"[37] according to World Vision's statement. "It will continue to discuss the possibility of re-starting work under any new legal

---

[36] Ibid
[37] Ibid

framework which the government may subsequently introduce."

We can see that international organizations are working in Pakistan, and they are helping the life of people who are in need. They report on the human right abuse in Pakistan in front of the international community. The effect of blasphemy law that is prevalent of Pakistan is felt by those international organizations. However, due to the threat of mobs and religious leaders in Pakistan, they cannot do anything except be mere spectators of the oppression of the people. The work done by the international organizations has been effective in rural areas in the field of education and poverty reductions, but the fight against the blasphemy law is not done by those organizations, and we can say that they have done next to nothing to improve the human rights situations of Pakistan. Local organizations, which claim themselves as the human rights organizations, are also nothing but the mouthpiece of the religious organizations and the political parties.

PART 5

Worship in the Valley of the Shadow of Death

Despite the pressure from the society and political situation of Pakistan, the Christians in Pakistan have been an oasis in the desert providing fertile soil for the growth of churches. The faith community of Pakistan is one of the strongest of believers in Christ. The forces from all sides try to stop the growth of Christians, and government is in full force to stop the growth of the church, but we can see that the number of Christians in Pakistan is increasing, along with the number of churches.

Baptism in Pakistan photo courtesy of mission network news (FMI).

PART 5: Worship in the valley of the shadow of death

Christian rallies during Easter

Christian seminaries in Pakistan

Even though Pakistan is among the list of the toughest countries for Christians, Jesus Christ is being glorified there, and God is moving. In Pakistan, we have very old seminaries, which have been raising Christian leaders. My school is one of them. We are raising mission-minded leaders and providing them two year ministry diplomas. This school was a result of a vision and a burden to raise leaders for this nation where training one person can bring many changes. We started training leaders through this school and seminars where local teachers teach, and we invite teachers from all over the world as well. We are making disciples in all over Pakistan. After finishing their training, these leaders and disciples are being sent into cities and remote and rural areas of Pakistan.

Christian evangelism and outreach

Evangelism is being done in different ways. There are some open-air crusades being organized by local and foreign preachers, and they are preaching the gospel in different cities and areas of Pakistan. Some Christian TV channels are also busy spreading the gospel. Some groups are reaching the unreached areas with the gospel. Our ministry is much concerned to reach the unreached areas and the lost. We have been doing outreach to remote and northern areas of Pakistan. It is a big challenge to do outreach and reaching the lost. But God has been using His people to share the gospel. It is not easy. There is no freedom to share the gospel. Still, He is being witnessed in Pakistan where 97% of the population is Muslim. As Pakistani Christians, we have very strong faith in Jesus Christ, in spite of all our suffering and persecution, and we never compromise on our faith and in giving testimony. Nothing can stop us from worshipping Him and witnessing of Him in Pakistan.

Evangelism in Pakistan is not an easy task by any means. In the midst of hostility, church planting is a dangerous proposition, especially when seminary training is not always available to all the pastors and evangelists.

While keeping the perilous conditions, pastors and evangelists in Pakistan face harsh antagonism as they go about planting churches. Nonetheless, Pakistani Christians are keen to share the gospel with others in the face of potential backlash from the Islamic fundamentalists. While this remains, there is a solid reality that pastors and evangelists receive threats in order to deter them

PART 5: Worship in the Valley of the Shadow of Death

International Preachers in Pakistan

Audio video lab for evangelism in Pakistan

from spreading the faith. Seeing this, Forgotten Missionaries International (FMI) has called upon all to pray for the pastors and evangelists who are working in the predominantly Muslim nation—Pakistan.

In this regard, Bruce Allen from the Forgotten Missionaries International (FMI) says, "Christian pastors are getting death threats from folks saying, 'We know who you are. We know where you are. Prepare to die within a matter of days.' "[38]

---

[38] https://www.mnnonline.org/news/conference-spotlight-church-planting-in-restrictive-countries/

Church planting

Many people think that Christianity is blocked or illegal in countries like China or North Korea, and Christianity is legal in Pakistan. But the reality is that Christianity is under threat in Pakistan more than anywhere else. In spite of that, it is still possible to plant churches in Pakistan with the help of Almighty God. Many people have asked me if you could build churches in Pakistan. My answer is yes.

Building churches in Pakistan is allowed. This is the reason I am writing this book. Many people do not know the inside situation of Pakistan Christianity, and I want to highlight the reality behind being Christians in Pakistan. Christianity is legal in Pakistan, even though we do not have freedom and safety. Despite the hardships,

Christian churches are being built there, and new churches are planted every now and then.

We can build churches, and it is a vision of my ministry to build 100 churches by 2030 in Pakistan. This is another example of worshiping in the valley of the shadow of death. God is using His people to build churches, and

Church building project

many new churches have been planted the last few years. It is our prayer that Christians can worship in those churches and worship Almighty God in Pakistan. In the wake of these issues like security and blasphemy law, church planting becomes a lot more difficult and stressful where the population is predominantly hostile toward the Christian faith. Nonetheless, the pastors, the evangelists, the church planters are fully aware of the culture in which we serve.

These valiant pastors and evangelists understand the rewards they are to get after all the striving as they continue to press on amidst intense persecution and hostility. Pakistan is a country where blasphemy law can easily be implied to entangle a Christian even though any "substantial" evidence of the "blasphemy" is available or not. Moreover, not only the pastors and evangelists who are in trouble, but their families suffer also.

Christians and Christianity in Pakistan are a guarantee of blessing and progress

Prime Minister of Pakistan, Imran Khan, stated in an Islamic convention that there is no mention of Jesus Christ in the history of the world. It shows his lack of knowledge of history and his knowledge about Jesus Christ, the most transformational leader in the history of mankind. Somehow, if a Christian had stated that about the Prophet of Islam, it would be an act of blasphemy. This statement has been condemned by many Muslim journalists who know history on TV channels of Pakistan. I would say it hurts Christians as well, but we do not make it a matter of life and death. But the truth is, this world has been made new by Jesus Christ. History cannot and will never be complete without Jesus Christ. History is His-story.

"And he that sat upon the throne said, Behold, I make all things new. And he said unto me, Write: for these words are true and faithful." (Rev. 21:5 KJV)

Some people have made transformational changes in one department of human learning or in one aspect of human life. And their names are forever enshrined in the annals of human history. However, Jesus Christ, the greatest Man who ever lived, has changed virtually every aspect of human life, and most people do not know it.

Jesus says in Revelation 21:5, *"Behold, I make all things new."* In Greek *behold* means "Note well," "look closely," "examine carefully." It shows that we must pay close attention.

I. Jesus is the force of the transformation of this world

Everything that Jesus Christ touched He transformed. Jesus is a transformational leader. He touched time when he was born into this world. He had a birthday, and that birthday utterly changed the way we measure time. Now, the whole world counts time as Before Christ (B.C.) and Anno Domini (A.D.), "In the year of the Lord."

Jesus was the most transformational leader; he has influenced the most in his three years' ministry. Socrates, Plato, Aristotle lived 130 years, and they did not influenced people as Jesus did. Jesus preached for only three years, and today, out of three people in the world one is Christian. He never wrote any book; however, today, most of the books are about Him. He never wrote any poetry, but today, so much poetry is about Jesus. Jesus never traveled out of Israel; today, you can see Christians in every part of the world. He never painted any pictures, but today, you can see a lot of paintings of Jesus. Almost every big painter painted him.

Wherever Christianity penetrated, those nations were radically changed. They became civilized societies. Christianity has shaped the European culture. Today, it is a dream of many people to go to Europe and get settled there. America became a great country because of Christians and the gospel. Christians made America a great country. America's Constitution is full of Bible verses. I am sure Pakistan needs more Christians, and the gospel should be preached there more. Therefore, Pakistan can be a great country. Jesus has power to transform the societies and nations. He makes all things new.

II. The world is beautiful due to Jesus

Jesus has changed this world. Christ and Christians have made this world a beautiful place. Here, I would like to add the summary of a book by James Kennedy and Jerry Newcombe[39] on how the world have benefitted from the arrival of Jesus Christ and how he has managed to change the face of the earth. The deeds of Christ are unfathomable, and this transformative force can be useful in changing the society of Pakistan.

1. The humanity and humanism has changed since the arrival of Jesus.

Prior to the introduction of Jesus Christ, human life on this planet was modest. Indeed, even today, in numerous pieces of the existence where the good news of Christ or Christianity has not infiltrated, life is exceedingly modest. In any case, Jesus Christ—He who says, "Be-

---

[39] D. James Kennedy and Jeremy Newcombe, *What If Jesus Had Never Been Born?* (Nashville, Tennessee: Thomas Nelson, 2001).

hold, I make everything new," gave humankind another point of view on the estimation of human life. In the antiquated world, individuals were utilized to forfeit their kids. Jesus stated, "Let the little kids come to me..." Christianity has raised the lady. Before Jesus it dislike that ladies were dealt with gravely. Christianity nullified bondage. Generally, there were numerous slaves on the planet, even in USA, too, (read Philemon), and Christianity has debilitated suicide. In 4000 years history of book of Scriptures, just seven individuals ended it all. Basic entitlements, before Christianity, it was not as you see today. This is the appropriate response: I provided for my Muslim companion who needed me to acknowledge Islam. I can't perceive any preferred pioneer over Jesus Christ. I accept that the world needs Jesus more than everything else. Jesus can make everything new. The entire planet is nothing without Jesus.

2. *Compassion and Mercy*

Christianity added to support poor people. Jesus, who rose from the dead, set the extraordinary case of helping poor people, of thinking about the neediness of the stricken. The anecdote of the Good Samaritan is a perfect example, (Luke 10:25-37). The education provided by Jesus has presented the possibility of "Christ's poor," Matt. 25:40. Most of the philanthropy today is done for the sake of Christ, all NGOs, Charity associations like World Vision International, Samaritan's Handbag, Christian Kids Help Support, Compassion International are working for the sake of Christ. It is a direct result of Christ and Christianity. Remove Jesus and you remove Santa Claus, which is a legendary character that indicates back to Christ. Santa speaks to empathy and leniency in the type of presents. It is said that history is His-Story. Remove Jesus from the history; it won't be history.

3. World became more Enlightened due to the teachings of Jesus

Jesus Christ has enlightened the world and its population in one way or another. Before the advent of Jesus Christ, the world was a dark place, but after His arrival, the world has become lighter. If we see the examples of Europe and America, the populations were ignorant, as education was only available for the royalties and high class people. But with the arrival of the gospel and message of Jesus Christ, the education came together with it. When we take the examples of many universities around the world, we can see that the darkness of ignorance has been wiped away with the educational light of Christ. The schools that are established by the missionaries are still top schools in their respective countries in different parts of the world. So we can claim that Jesus is the foundation of education all over the world.

Whatever the world has today, it is because of Jesus Christ, and Christians have given universities to Pakistan. Pakistan has been benefitted by Christianity and Christians. This country needs more Jesus; this country should respect Jesus and Christianity. This is my prayer that our education standard could be like those developed countries who accepted Christianity. We need to be more open for the gospel. This is the way Pakistan can improve their education standard. Pakistan needs Jesus Christ who makes all things new.

4. Democratic values in the governance can be attributed to Jesus

Christianity has promoted democracy, and Christianity itself is a beautiful example of democracy. John Calvin talked about democracy. Christianity gave democracy to America. Today, America is enjoying the benefits of democracy. Democracy in Pakistan is not the real democracy. This country does not practice democracy. There is also no democracy in the political parties. Sometimes Pakistani Prime minister is very confused when he says we want Pakistan like (Ryast-e-Medina) and glorifies democracy in England and the West.

There was no democracy in Ryast-e Medina. Even today in Saudi Arabia, there is kingship, not democracy. Prime Minster also glorifies China, and in China, there is no democracy at all. Therefore, we must learn church and Christianity is an institution to learn democracy. Pakistan needs church and Christians. Today, no prominent Christian's name is in government who can play his role in the development of Pakistan. It is sad. The government does not believe that a Christian can also make this country a better country.

5. Freedom for all

The world is enjoying freedom because of Jesus Christ. I feel that Pakistan also needs Jesus to enjoy freedom. We got freedom from British August 14, 1947, but people have not felt the real meaning of freedom and liberty. Through Jesus Christ, this world has experienced amazing grace (John 1:14). Jesus was full of grace and truth.

This word "grace" shaped the European culture. Jesus was the most attractive person in the world, and Christianity is the most attractive religion. Jesus loved people who never deserved love. Jesus was used to eating and drinking with sinners. In Matthew 9, Jesus told that He came for the sick, not for those who are healthy. Jesus forgave the woman who was caught in the crime of adultery. Jesus forgave the criminal on the cross who never did good works and was not going to do good works after his death. It was just grace. Grace is not fair; it is better than fair. Pakistan needs to experience the grace of Jesus Christ.

Pakistan is an Islam country where 97% of the people are Muslims. Pakistan is a poor country because its roots are not in Christianity, and this is the reason we do not have human rights, freedom, democracy, education, compassion, and civilized society, though Pakistan has many resources. However, the resources are not utilized due to the lack of good governance and knowledge. To make the proper utilization of those resources, the enlightenment of Jesus is necessary, and people should have liberty to use those resources, which can only be possible through Jesus. Wherever Christianity penetrated, those nations and countries became prosperous and civilized. My professor in ACTS, Korea was used to teach us that Korea has become a rich country because of the Gospel, and 70% of good works or welfare is done by the church in Korea. Korea's progress is a miracle for the world.

Conclusion

The resurrected Jesus has changed this world because of Jesus Christ who was born, died, and raised again from the dead. Risen Jesus is the reason for everything in this world. He can make all things new. He can touch and make our relationships new. He can change our bad financial life and make it new. He is expert in changing te lives. I believe that He is hope for the world and for Pakistan. If Christianity had been accepted and treated well in Pakistan, situations could be different in Pakistan. I do pray that their eyes open and they seek Jesus Christ.

Due to the marginalization of the minorities like Christians by the government and the society, most Christians in Pakistan are living difficult lives of poverty in slum areas. That is not stopping them from rejoicing in the Lord. The persecutions faced by the Christians in Pakistan can be related to the persecutions faced by the churches in the early church eras. Similar stance of killing, harassing, and torturing can be seen in everyday life. However, in spite of all those hardships, the Christians are getting stronger in their faith.

According to *NBC News*, most of the city's Christians can be found living in ramshackle houses constructed over open sewers in ghettos hidden from sight behind whitewashed walls. Authorities supply no power or gas to the slums, which are essentially cities within cities and in some cases are nestled between Islamabad's most plush neighborhoods.[40]

Poverty is not the choice of Christians. They are some of the hardest working people in Pakistan, but they are forced into poverty. Many Christians in the past were wealthy and had many properties in their name, but in recent times, those properties have been taken by the Muslim people in some pretexts. Being a wealthy Christian is to be the target of many who despise them.

The rights of people was guaranteed in the constitution, and being a citizen, all Pakistanis are equal on paper, but in practice, Christians are considered as second-class citizens. Anybody can press charge against Christians and can take their properties, and nobody dares to complain against such acts. This has violated the words of the founder of Pakistan.
Pakistan's founder, Mohammad Ali Jinnah, proclaimed in 1947 that his fellow citizens "may belong to any reli-

---

[40] https://www.nbcnews.com/news/world/why-it-feels-crime-be-christian-pakistan-n179511

gion or caste or creed and that has nothing to do with the business of the state."[41] But his sayings are just in words as no practice of the equality of all people in spite of faith, race, and religion is implemented. The voice of the minority Christians are hardly heard by the society and the people in power.

Even though the condition of Christians in Pakistan is very sorrowful there, there is unity and respect among themselves. They have respect for the Pastors and vision of churches, so they unite in planting new churches and give guidance to the new Christians. Because of that, we can see gradual growth in the numbers of churchgoers and the growth of numbers of churches in different parts of the country.

Lahore, a city in Punjab hails the highest numbers of Christians in Pakistan. The population of Christians in Lahore is estimated to be around 4,000,000, a significant growth from the past ten years. This signifies the church growth is difficult situation in Pakistan. This growth can be found in other parts of the country, too, like in the Gujranwala and Karachi.

Even though the condition of Christians in Pakistan is not good, the work of Christians can be recognized by the society as a whole. The harmonious and peaceful natures of Christians have many hearts and the help that they are providing to the community is taken positively by the society.
Christians have been able to help their needy neighbors when they are struggling. Pakistan has basic problems of drinking

---

[41] Ibid

water, but many churches dig their own wells and have provided drinking water facilities to the local areas. Not only that, but when natural disasters and other emergencies occur, Christians are the first to run for emergency aids.

Because of this nature of Christians in Pakistan, some portions of Pakistan society applaud them, even though in silence. For example, in Pakistani society, it is considered that Christians are very honest people and do not lie and do not steal? Many Muslims admit this, and many families prefer Christian workers. It is also a fact that many Muslim families prefer to have Christian teachers for their kids for home tuition. Christians have played very important roles in education.

Challenges faced by the Christian Community besides persecution

For the further growth of churches and Christians in Pakistan, it is better to look at some of the challenges that are faced by the Christians in Pakistan. First challenge for the Christians in Pakistan is the lack of political activities by any Christians. This might happen because of ignorance of the people and the pressure from the majority groups, but it is a pitiful condition that many Pakistani Christian youngsters are not interested in the political matter of the country. They have a lack of knowledge on what political activities can do to improve their livelihood. The world has changed, and youths all around the world seek solutions for the problem through democratic criteria, but it is opposite in the case of Pakistani Christian youth. The non-Christian youths are active in the political activities and are up to date with the things that are going on around them, but this is not seen in the Christian youth. The improvement of livelihood of Christians in Pakistan can be greatly transformed if the youth and other Christians in Pakistan overcome this challenge.

At this point, we cannot see any prominent Christian leaders in politics, and those who are in politics are not the leaders. They are the servants of political parties who select them after coming into power. Whenever they get a chance to speak, they do not speak for Christians. They speak for their parties who select them.

The second challenge that Christians in Pakistan should overcome is the stigma that they have been attached with as being an underprivileged class of people. Christians should not present themselves as underprivileged and should try to be of equal status with other Pakistanis. When a person claims that he is underprivileged and seeks help from others, that kind of person will never come up and attain the equal status as privileged people. Christians know that there is nobody to help them when they are in need. Then why should they wait for the government and other responsible authorities to uplift them? They should raise themselves up. This is a very challenging prospect, but if this step is not taken in time, then they will have to wait for a long time to be out of the group of underprivileged people.

Jesus is the only one that we have who can answer for our lives. There is nobody above Jesus, and with His power, Christians in Pakistan can be independent and do not have to be underprivileged forever. Many institutions and organizations as well as universities and schools are run on Christian principles. It requires a will and the courage of Christians in Pakistan to learn different vocations and utilize those vocations for agriculture, businesses, and other necessary things. If that is accomplished, then Christians in Pakistan can be independent sooner, and they can overcome the taboo of being underprivileged. This challenge is not difficult to overcome if the Christians realize the power of self with the help of Christ.

The next challenge that Christians in Pakistan need to overcome is the challenge of assimilation and integration with other groups of people. Christians in Pakistan mostly tend to live in their own clusters and have very little or no interaction with their Muslim counterparts. The local communities know very little about the Christians and their problem due to these self-isolations. Because of their seclusion, many Christians are not involved in social activities. If they get out of their own milieu and get more active in social activities as marriage, festival celebrations, and other social issues, this can create an opportunity for Christians to be part of the society.

It is imperative that responsible Christian organizations should encourage Christians to participate in such events. There might be some social barriers for doing so, but if it is not initiated, then the things will always remain the same, and there will be no change for a long time to come. Human behavior is the same in all ,and society will gradually accept the presence of Christians among them if these kinds of activities are started. Social harmony is necessary to bring about the change in the country, and Christians in Pakistan should not stay behind in seclusion for bringing about such changes.

Conclusion

Finally, Christians in Pakistan should be competent in modern technological advances. If a person in today's age are lagging behind in the technological terms and uses, then that person will miss a lot of things. Christians in Pakistan should come forward and learn about the technological world. Christians in Pakistan are really behind in such important subjects as technology, and if they remain so, then there will never be advancement in the society.

Steps should be taken to overcome these challenges. The persecutions are there, and blasphemy law is always hanging on over the head of Christians, but the challenges mentioned above are the challenges that can be overcome by one's own efforts. If the steps to overcoming these challenges are taken seriously and churches are ready to help the congregation in overcoming those challenges, then we can see a different face of Christianity in Pakistan in coming days.

Churches can get involved in social works and can provide some educational scholarships, vocational training, and support facilities to the needy children of the area. That can gain more attraction toward the work of Christians and can gain good will among the people.

Many more activities can be done from churches, like funding in local businesses and giving new ideas on agriculture and animal rearing. This way, churches can play an important role in the economy of the society. Once the church is involved in important economic cycles of the society, it can get more traction for growth.

1. Every Christian church should sponsor a clean well, so they do not need to go to Muslim wells to get water. Instead of that, Muslims should come to Christian's wells to get clean water.

2. Humanitarian needs for persecuted Christians.

3. Relief aid for persecuted Christians, privacy for worship, freedom for worship, there should be media system that can inform what is happening to Christians.

4. Funds should be set up for safe havens to help persecuted Christians.

5. Christian aid to rescue people who are suffering because of persecution.

6. International reporter to report what's going on.

Am I my brother's keeper? Jesus said to love your neighbor as yourself. We are one family. Has the world forgotten Christians in Pakistan?

Questions need to be presented to the world about Christians in Pakistan and answered about how the world is going to help.

Final Words

The blasphemy law in Pakistan is killing the society in one way or another. The incidents that have happened in different parts of Pakistan, which we read about in this book, are the result of this awful law. I stress that this law should be revised so that all the minorities, including some of the Muslim minorities, can breathe of peaceful air. Christians are persecuted in every corner of Pakistan due to this law.

Jesus Christ, however, encourages His disciples to be the light of the world. Light is very important for life. Christians in Pakistan want to be light in their society and bring the people in darkness toward the light. But the efforts of Christians in Pakistan alone cannot be enough to bring the light to the dark alleys of Pakistan.

We, the Christians in Pakistan, need encouragement and prayers from our Christian brothers and sisters in the places where the darkness is already won by the light. You have the comfort of living in a free society and practicing your faith without any fear. But we need your support in prayer for that growth in our part of the world.

We thank you.

BIBLIOGRAPHY

Cited Websites and Materials

Page

23 [1] https://www.europarl.europa.eu/sides/getDoc.do?pubRef=//EP//TEXT+WQ+E-1998-2021+0+DOC+XML+V0//EN

23 [2] http://news.bbc.co.uk/onthisday/hi/dates/stories/october/28/newsid_2478000/2478093.stm

23 [3] https://www.telegraph.co.uk/news/worldnews/asia/pakistan/1388121/Five-killed-as-grenades-are-thrown-into-church.html *Five killed as grenades are thrown into church.* (3/18/2002)

23 [4] http://news.bbc.co.uk/2/hi/south_asia/2173184.stm *Gunmen attack Pakistan school.* (8/5/2002)

24 [5] http://www.asianews.it/news-en/Sangla-Hill-tragedy:-victims-speak-out-a-year-later-7748.html *Sangla Hill tragedy: victims speak out a year later.* (11/14/2006)

25 [6] https://www.bbc.com/news/world-asia-35909677 *Pakistan Taliban faction claims park attack on Lahore Christians* (3/26/2016)

30 [7] https://www.nytimes.com/2017/12/17/world/asia/pakistan-quetta-church-attack.html *Pakistan Church Attacked by 2 Suicide Bombers* (12/17/2017)

35 [8] These are the excerpts of incidents that harmed the Christians in Pakistan that took place only in 2018. There are innumerable accounts in the past years where the Christians are persecuted here in one way or other. Some of the major incidents are discusses in the following parts. The incidents are taken from different online sources and all of them are the part of citation, however not all the online outlets were remembered as these were recorded in the written form after they were found online. It is my regret to not include all of them here, but I thank them all for bringing out the pain that Christians of Pakistan suffer in their own home turf.
Most of the lists of incidents quoted here are taken from the website: www.persecution.org

37 [9] The full story can be found at: https://www.ucanews.com/news/muslims-accused-of-raping-christian-teenager-in-pakistan/85441

40 [10] http://www.wafpak.org/pages/christianity%20in%20pakistan.html

43 [11] https://www.washingtonpost.com/news/worldviews/wp/2016/03/28/the-plight-of-pakistans-christian-minority/ *An Easter Sunday suicide bombing shows plight of Pakistan's Christians*, Adam Taylor 3/28/2016

44 [12] https://web.archive.org/web/20091110133919/http://www.pakistani.org/pakistan/constitution/part3.ch3.notes.html *Constitution of Pakistan*

47 [13] https://tribune.com.pk/story/1016235/islamabads-christian-slum-dwellers-pray-for-christmas-miracle/ *Islamabad's Christian slum dwellers pray for Christmas miracle.* By AFP. Published: 12/25/2015

Bibliography

49	[14]	https://www.ucanews.com/news/muslims-accused-of-raping-christian-teenager-in-pakistan/85441 *Muslims accused of raping Christian teenager in Pakistan*
52	[15]	Shafique Khokhar, Asianews.it, 7/12/2019
54	[16]	https://webcache.googleusercontent.com/search?q=cache:2YRbfwMXJ2EJ:https://www.opendoors.no/Admin/Public/Download.aspx%3Ffile%3DFiles%252FFiles%252FNO%252FWWL-2018-dokumenter%252FPakistan-Church-Facts-and-History.pdf+&cd=1&hl=en&ct=clnk&gl=kr *WWL 2018 Church History & Facts – PAKISTAN*
	[17]	This has been reported in the world Christian database and available in https://worldchristiandatabase.org/
55	[18]	http://www.columbia.edu/itc/mealac/pritchett/00islamlinks/txt_jinnah_assembly_1947.html *Muhammad Ali Jinnah's first Presidential Address to the Constituent Assembly of Pakistan* (8/11/1947)
57	[19]	https://www.christiansinpakistan.com/christianity-in-pakistan/ *Christianity in Pakistan*
60	[20]	Ibid
61	[21]	https://www.bbc.com/news/world-asia-48204815 *What are Pakistan's blasphemy laws?* 5/8/2019
62	[22]	Ibid
69	[23]	https://www.bbc.co.uk/news/resources/idt-sh/Asia_Bibi *Asia Bibi Pakistan's notorious blasphemy case*
72	[24]	https://www.theguardian.com/world/2011/mar/02/pakistan-minister-shot-dead-islamabad *Pakistan minister Shahbaz Bhatti shot dead in Islamabad.* 3/2/2011
78	[25]	https://barnabasfund.org/en/news/mentally-disabled-christian-man-charged-with-blasphemy-in-pakistan *Mentally disabled Christian man charged with "blasphemy" in Pakistan*
79	[26]	*A Peaceful Struggle*, Ed. Fr. Khalid Rashid ASI. Box 87, G.P.O., Bishop's House, Faisalabad, Pakistan, May 1999, p. 111
85	[27]	https://www.pakistanchristianpost.com/opinion-details/3315 *Attacks on Shantinagar and Khanewal: RAMIFICATIONS OF PAKISTAN BLASPHEMY LAWS*
87	[28]	https://www.bbc.com/news/world-asia-42383436 *Deadly attack on Methodist church in Pakistan.* 12/18/2017
88	[29]	https://www.bbc.com/news/world-asia-35909677 *Pakistan Taliban faction claims park attack on Lahore Christians.* 3/28/2016
92	[30]	https://www.dawn.com/news/877158
93	[31]	Ibid
96	[32]	https://www.vice.com/gr/article/dp4q5m/blasphemy-laws-in-pakistan-provide-cover-for-all-kinds-of-grudges *The Joseph Colony Fire: Blasphemy Laws in Pakistan Provide Cover for All Kinds of Grudges.* 3/18/2013

Bibliography

[33] Ibid

98   [34] https://www.hrw.org/world-report/2019/country-chapters/pakistan
Pakistan Events of 2018

101 [35] https://www.christianitytoday.com/news/2018/december/world-vision-out-of-pakistan-international-charities-ngos.html
World Vision Forced Out of Pakistan After 13 Years. 12/20/2018

102 [36] Ibid

[37] Ibid

107 [38] https://www.mnnonline.org/news/conference-spotlight-church-planting-in-restrictive-countries/ *Conference to spotlight church planting in restrictive countries.* 1/7/2016

112 [39] Kennedy, D. James and Jeremy Newcombe. *What If Jesus Had Never Been Born?* Nashville, Tennessee: Thomas Nelson, 2001.

118 [40] https://www.nbcnews.com/news/world/why-it-feels-crime-be-christian-pakistan-n179511 *Why It Feels Like a "Crime" to Be Christian in Pakistan.* 8/15/2014

119 [41] Ibid

www.ingramcontent.com/pod-product-compliance
Lightning Source LLC
Chambersburg PA
CBHW070201100426
42743CB00013B/3005